THE
PROFESSIONAL WRITERS'
PHRASE BOOK

THE
PROFESSIONAL
WRITERS'
PHRASE
BOOK

JEAN KENT

A PERIGEE BOOK

Perigee Books
are published by
The Putnam Publishing Group
200 Madison Avenue
New York, NY 10016

Book design by The Sarabande Press

Typeset by Fisher Composition, Inc.

Library of Congress Cataloging-in-Publication Data

Kent, Jean Salter.
Professional writers' phrase book.

Companion volume to: The romance writers'
phrase book / Jean S. Kent.
"A Perigee book."
1. Authorship—Handbooks, manuals, etc.
2. English language—Terms and phrases.
I. Kent, Jean Salter. Romance writers'
phrase book.   II. Title.
PN147.K425   1987   808.3   86-25128
ISBN 0-399-51338-8

Printed in the United States of America
1   2   3   4   5   6   7   8   9   10

CONTENTS

Contents

INTRODUCTION

"Show, don't tell," is advice that most writers have heard ever since they wrote their "What I Did Last Summer" essay in the fourth grade. Though the advice is good, it's also contradictory, because it's telling, not showing, exactly what we want to avoid.

This book is for writers who, like myself, have to be SHOWN. We all agree that words don't mean anything unless they conjure up pictures, but how do we go about creating these pictures? The answer is, by using descriptive phrases, or, as I call them, tags. What, exactly, is a tag? Instead of telling you, I'll show you.

Suppose you want to add:

1. More color:
   Original Script: The garden was full of flowers.
   Revised Script: The white mums frilled themselves in the warm sun.
2. More expression:
   Original script: She smiled at him.
   Revised script: She gave him a rare, intimate smile, beautiful with brightness.
3. More meaning:
   Original script: He spoke haltingly.

Revised script: He was barely able to wheeze through his prepared speech.

I'm sure you'll agree that the revised script is much more descriptive, and that's very nice but, you say, that's only three tags—nowhere near enough. You need hundreds of them. You've got them.

This book contains over 3,500 descriptive phrases covering the most frequently traveled areas of writing. For fiction writers, for example, "Body Movements" shows you how to make your people move. "Environment" shows you how to set the mood. "Personality Traits" will help you add depth to your characters. The purpose of this book, however, is not to give you a lot of phrases you can copy verbatim, but to teach you how to create your own phrases.

Though many of the tags in this book can be used in copywriting as well as in creative writing, there are many phrases that are for copywriters only. I call these "trade tags." Some of them form the end sections in the book and are noted in the contents under this title. There is also a section called *Product Promotion*. Next to "Sex," it's the largest category in the book and the most specialized. It's intended to give you suggestions that will help jazz up your copy. For example, if you were writing a jewelry ad, instead of:

Original copy: The quality is guaranteed.
Revised copy: Create a niche in your life for the one perfect thing.

An ad for a restaurant:

Original copy: We specialize in gourmet cooking.
Revised copy: Revel in the unexpected.

For businessmen who need pep-talk phrases, there's the *Incentive and Motivation* section. These tags are suitable for speeches, bulletin board notices, intra-company memos, or even locker room discussions at halftime.

They're all here, the words and the power behind them. It's up to you to adapt them to your style of writing. Familiarize yourself with all the tags in the book. They are tools, and like all good tools, unless you learn how to use them, they're no good to you. Find the tags you like and rewrite them to suit your needs. After you've done this for a while, you'll begin to develop a feeling for the mood and tone of your work and then the creative juices will start to flow.

This is a workbook, so use it accordingly. Make notes in it. Mark it up. Rearrange it. Jot down new ideas in the margins. Draw arrows between phrases you want to mix/match. The point is, put this book to work for you . . . and you'll soon realize it's the most valuable tool you have.

—*Jean Salter Kent*

he decided to dispense with the pleasantries and meet fire with fire

but she was pushing words across to him now

it was a throwaway accusation, but she'd hit home

then came a well-measured response

knowing his words had the power to wound

time to bring out the heavy artillery

all right, let's get into it

but he went on gamely

the last obstacles fell away

she gave him a most unladylike dustup

if I hold it in any longer, I'll blow out my teeth

after an equally insulting pause . . .

a sudden declaration of war between them

the carefully rehearsed defense attack has escalated into outright war

the words were sudden and raw and very angry

feisty as all hell

confused and crazily furious

she said, with a note of sulky truculence

she replied bitingly

angry because he'd forced her to behave in an uncivil fashion

the maddening inability to break free

. . . certainly no welcome in THIS greeting

kept alive by a deep-buried fire of anger that never goes out

she hung up before he could come up with a smooth reply

the rage in him was a living thing

violence bubbled

their tempers at flash point

his long nose pinched and white with resentful rage

the anger hanging in the air between them like an invisible dagger

their eyes locked in open warfare

she blazed tightly

his face became red and blotchy with anger

blood-chilling anger

his anger was controlled but more dangerous than usual

fury lurked beneath the smile

she blazed right up at him

she cried, flashing into sudden fury

their eyes traded strings of malevolence

she turned on him with a sudden flash of defensive spirit

like an awakening giant

LIMBS

hooked her thumb in her panties and cocked her hip

laced her fingers around his neck

he swatted her behind

pectoral muscles in perfect colloquy with the movement of his arms

he slipped her hand through the crook of his arm and squeezed her to him

bowing slightly from the waist, he gestured toward the door with a flourishing wave of his arm

he patted his shirt in an absent, searching gesture

raised his glass in concession

with an affectionate slap on the flank

raised his hands in a don't-shoot pose

giving him a slight nudge in the ribs

he cocked his arm

he threw his arms up, fists balled

brushed back some hair that the wind had caressed out of place

raising the tea cup to his heavily mustached lips

approaching with a smile and an outstretched hand

as she talked she rubbed her hands on her arms and paced

arms folded tightly

he put his arms around her waist and pushed her up the stairs

he left the bar, sketching a farewell wave to . . .

her arms wrapped around her pillow like a child holding a favorite doll

talking with wide sweeps of his arms

his pointing arm was serpentine

crossed her leg and swung her upper limb impatiently

he reached for the cord and drew the blind

fanned themselves with cardboard-revival fans

with vigorous congratulations, thumpings on the back, terrific shakings of the hand

she newspapered each knickknack before packing it away

he raised his hands in a primitive gesture of reassurance

reaching over, he knuckled the boy's head

he banged the guy on the back

slamming the hammerhead into the springy white planks

he held the paper just out of her reach

clutching a ragged brown package against his thigh

he scrubbed his curly gray hair with his knuckles

he slammed his swivel chair level

undressing, he paused a moment, sock in hand

he snatched the key and flipping it over his back, caught it in his right hand and bounced it in his palm

with a thud he slapped his fist into his other hand

wiping the corners of his eyes with the back of his hand

twisting her handkerchief in her lap

he fanned the air with his hands in disgust

she kneaded the stiff muscles with one hand and rolled her head in a circle

clinching his hands against the bottoms of his pockets

his hands rested on the desk, motionless, like empty gloves

he stroked the cheek beside him with great tender fingers

flipped a palm back and forth

wagging his finger like a teacher, sure in his dogma

he framed the match with his hand

he ran his hands through his hair in a detached motion

drummed the desk top with his pen

pointing his pipe like a pistol

he said, with a cautionary lift of his hand

one thick hand pinched a cigarette

his fingers trembled in an attitude of grasping

flinging his hands up in a halting gesture

then tossed it up in his hands, speculatively

he made a circle of thumb and forefinger to tell him he had won

he slapped his hands together explosively

a hand descended on his shoulder from behind

holding his hands behind his immense back

kissed his bunched up fingers . . . MNYEH!

a moth-wind flutter of her hand

combing her hair back with the fingers of both hands

poking his fists into the pockets of his Levi's

lacing his fingers with hers

placing his two forefingers together, he pressed them against his lips

he took it with the tips of his fingers

cupped his mouth with his hands and sucked in his breath

nervously rubbed her fingernails with her thumb

dusted his hands together

thumbs hitched in his belt

made a tent of strong, hairy fingers

settled his elbows on the desk and steepled his fingers

he hooked a thumb in the direction of the road

almost overpowering handshake

slapped his head

picked up the whiskey and knocked it back

adjusted the jets of water by spinning the dial of the shower

arcing his arm through the air, he gestured at their surroundings

lifting his hand in an emphatic gesture

his fingers tiptoed up her calf to her knee

gesturing broadly with his right arm

stroked her cheek with the back of his knuckles

he kissed his fingers

twisting the focus knobs on the binoculars

she looked where his finger led her

hooked one elbow over the backrest of his chair

bare feet spread and braced on the dock

hands behind his back, he stiffened his massive weight

paper-clipped the data into appropriate sheaves

he shifted his weight to his arms as if to rise

put his arms behind his head and rested back against his hands

his left forearm rested on his knee, his head hung forward

with his left arm across the back of the seat, he twisted around and said . . .

rotates a finger near his temple

talking nonstop, her hands gliding through the air

he held up a quieting hand

his hand moved with blurring speed

HEAD

"Yes," she said over her shoulder

scanning the room for somebody socially startling

after a second, reassuring glance backwards . . .

he twisted a benzedrine inhaler up a hairy nostril

he blew out his cheeks

he indicated the door with a jerk of his head as one is taught to do in the movies

she pushed her hair back, the better to glare at him

she screwed her face up and yelled . . .

stared upward and sniffed the heavens

patted a curl here and there

combing his strong black hair with his fingers

nodding a thank you

she asked over her shoulder

pulled back his shoulders and lifted his granite jaw

he held his head arrogantly back as though sniffing something

she sniffed with satisfaction at this arrangement

with a graceful toss of her head

thrusting his head forward, he strained to make out something a few yards ahead of him

swiveled his head to keep her in view

he shook his head, warning her off

and took a somewhat beery breath of fresh air

he lit a cigarette and eyed me through the flame of the match

wrinkled her nose

moved his head slightly to establish perspective

she rested her head on his shoulder and sighed unevenly

her head up, her arms folded tight as a gate

pinching his upper lip between his teeth

BODY IN MOTION

there was a stalking, purposeful intent in his walk

he hauled up his pants and crammed in the tails of his shirt

she got stiffly to her feet, leaning hard on her cane

he carried himself with vigor and grace

a vivacious quickness in her every movement

she slapped her sleeves to get rid of the crumbs

he caught her at the waist with both hands and swung her into the boat

he made a hand-leap over the wall

drove his clenched fist into his palm

all his gestures were outside and violent

grasped his tightly rolled umbrella like a sword

artists' fluid, powerful strokes

straightened his tie, rolled down his sleeves and slipped on his jacket

panted his way through the door

. . . taking her full weight as she flew into his arms

grabbing up her gown for the run to the kitchen

took the three steps in one movement and ran to the car on the same momentum

he put the drinks into mismatched glasses

turned with a quick snap of his thick shoulders

snapped his fingers in his face

all his movements were precise, expected

she ditted around past all the channels

shook open the newspaper

he braced himself and smartened his pace

rushing in lunatic flight toward destruction

the doors swung open and the girl spilled into the room

sitting there, coat opened, knees wide, he took up an awful lot of room

he sat on the porch and waved away the flies

a body so supple it twanged

I moved slowly, balancing my head carefully atop my neck

she wiped her arm across her nose

he moved like a slug

smoked a cigarette and dribbled ash down his vest

drove with a wrist draped limply over the steering wheel

she dragged on her cigarette as though sucking in oxygen

she clasped her hands around her ankles

she squeezed herself into the driver's seat

he sat down feebly, wrecked

he got up reluctantly, hating himself

he stood in the doorway, lighted against the black night

his movements were backlit by the light of the room

he grumbled to his feet and did as he was ordered

he stood alone on the stage, drinking the life-giving adoration

the slow-spitting and squatting men watched her covetously

standing at the lip of a hole

he was simply standing there, watching her

the gesture contained an intimacy she hadn't intended

his praying-mantis body curled over the desk

moved with glacial slowness

she walks like a construction worker

a loose-boned, easy gait

they moved in slow motion as if under water

he moved with the sure grace of a forest creature

he left, wrapping the rags of his dignity around him

he moved with the hard grace of one who had total control of himself

he moved with the swiftness of a great buck

moving with a quiet economy of effort unusual in a man so tall and muscularly built

he strolled slowly, blankly watching his boots crunch into the snow

he had to insinuate himself and his luggage through the crowded front door

she moved with graceful economy

she moved lightly but with enough hip-sway to pull her skirt in alternate directions

he walked briskly, elegant as a knife

he prowled the rug, arms behind his back

two soldiers marched sentry paths

he advanced with a portly waddle

searched the place like a woman looking for aisle twelve in the supermarket

light, earth-sprung athlete's gait

gave a Toyota-leap

she got up and left, her walk slow and swaying

clumping loudly in his calked boots

he gimped his way back through the crowd

shouldering his way through the crowd

he stalked toward her

a nudge here, a hip there, and an occasional light shove

even physically, he seemed to shrink

bending forward to get a glimpse of cleavage

sitting on a bench, haunch to haunch

motioning that I be seated on her left

moving to the security of the desk

arched eyebrows, hesitant shrug

she turned and waved, her smile long-range but very visible

the warm bulk of the woman sitting next to him urged his thighs nearer to the window

she adjusted to wakefulness

banged his walker noisily across the room

left the room like a scolded hound

she sat down, damp and dumpy and radiating bleakness

she coiled into the flickering shadows

slumped dejectedly into the couch and curled her feet under her

furtively they shadowed their way up the hill

with the skilled, patient hand of a craftsman

still beavering away . . .

he moved confidently, cleanly

he disappeared down the block, his back ramrod straight, his arms pumping like crazy

as quick and quiet as a ferret

a man who moved quickly

gave a whirling salute and stamped his feet in a left turn

she executed a playful pirouette

wrapped it up with expressway speed

giving him a hip-cocked pose

he bowed obsequiously

leaned his crossed arms atop a cement piling

hunching his shoulder, he bent his mind to the nub of the argument

her skirt tucked up, her hands on one knee

with her feet on the fender, she frowned into the fire

he leaned toward her with a casual air of ownership

planting an elbow on her upper knee, she rested her chin on her cupped hand

putting his hands on his hips, he bent his torso backwards until his spine cracked

leaning forward, she clasped her hands together like an eager child

she sat hunched on the edge of the king-sized bed

held her hand to her forehead, her chin almost resting on her chest

he leaned forward, resting one elbow hard on the arm of her chair

curled up in the chair as if withdrawing from the fear

he bent over the steering wheel, almost hugging it

tucked one leg under her

taking on that "Let's be reasonable" slouch

they all straightened their backs, like flowers rising on their stems in the morning

struck a heroic pose

"No," she said, then closed

he moved with stiff, brittle dignity

he backed up a hasty half-step

marching away smartly, head high, chest out, pace-stick in place

leaning toward her, he peered into her face as though studying a painting in a museum

he hunched over the catalog and examined it closely

he got up and stretched the ague from his shoulders

leaning back with excessive nonchalance

he slouched against the door as he drove

tilting her shoulders one way, her hips another

he bent forward, grasping his legs just above the knees

leaning toward her in a gentle, inquiring fashion

closing the door, she leaned her back against it

his body became taut, and he stood hovering over her, his hands on his hips

BODY MOTIONLESS

sat with the ramrod posture of a British brigadier

the men stood like posts, arms hanging rigid, all waiting

standing like a terrier waiting for attention

with a sudden stop, she stood riveted and faced him

rifles across their shoulders

stiffly sat in a straight-backed chair

facing him, but not looking directly at him

she sat in practiced repose, hands in lap, ankles crossed

he stood there with battleship solidity

his posture militant

in an Olympian detachment sort of pose

standing there with an indolent, tomcat grace

he just stood there in the hush

he remained uncomfortably still

stretched out like an old dog

a thin old man, frozen on the edge of the fallow fields forever

sagged against the door, appalled at herself

sat with sneakers angled on the floor like frogs' feet

he sat, right foot on left knee

he sat propped against a tree, panting from exertion

leaning against the bookcase, smoking

settled hip-shot against the corner of the desk

huddled in the water

TRADE TAGS

for strength training and body conditioning

to maintain a high level of muscle tone

bronzed and beautiful

slim, trim silhouettes

the massive chest of a body builder

body heat has gone hi-tech

a tropical tan even where it doesn't show

for strength, power and muscular endurance . . .

with great stability in the shoulder girdle

to tone and energize your muscles . . .

the envied body of a dancer

foundation-training in the iron game

highly visible in an alluring bikini

the ultimate goal in powerlifting

the perfectly toned body of a ballerina
all feminine, all natural, all you
a curve-for-curve fit
ease away muscle knots
workout wonders for everyone
relax your body's pressure points
stretch and breathe into your abdomen
maximum muscle flexibility

BUILDINGS

EXTERIOR

a graceless mausoleum, drab and cold

the building's quiet thrummings

standing at the window in sprays of dust

through the sunny arch of glass, he saw . . .

concrete and glass, rigid, unimaginative, ugly

a small nasty shed with a furtive look

dried-up wallpaper curled itself from the yellow plaster

she got into one of the slits of the revolving door

chimneys poked up from the factory rooftops

covered with a patina of dirt

outbuildings showed light between warped siding

tarpaper roofing flapped forlornly

sprained doors hung open

the paint had weathered out of the fading letters of the sign

the cone of porch light

flights of steps, darkened doorways, shuttered shops . . .

the stately house remained aloof to the anguish of its owner

a security system that had everything but a moat filled with alligators the soapstone step was only large enough for one person

the solidity of the building was disguised by a pink stucco finish

the ceiling was bloated with water

the house had the feeling of comfortable decay

the history of the house was shameful and glorious

a suspect motel named El Ranko

the house had loftiness, majesty, grandeur

a crummy twelve-unit resort hotel

it wasn't an ordinary building but a home

the sort of railroad flat you find in the ghettos

it was Victorian *in excelsis*

Trade Tags

all of its past glory is still there

versatile and dramatic in design

a Federal-style town house

the massive pyramidal style of the 1930s

a mission-style exterior

a soft red brick Vermont homestead

built with traditional Victorian-era elegance

a unique country residence built of mellow clapboard

the epitome in luxury, space, graciousness

a blend of French country and contemporary

a redwood home hidden beneath a sod roof

a custom-designed Spanish hacienda

an oceanfront masterpiece

snuggled into a hillside and surrounded by eucalyptus trees

a condo in a canyon

an equestrian ranch home with a New England flavor

a European villa with a crisp stucco façade

a dramatic fieldstone chateau

INTERIOR

the moon-wet sill

the apartment was clean and modern and pseudo something

the carpet wore a floral pattern

an opulent example of Chinese art

the air had been breathed too many times

sat at a table about as big as a diaper

rose-colored couches that faced each other

the sun-bombarded curtains were an anemic pink

over the years, the color of the pillows had polarized

the carpet was a shade of gray designed to hide dirt

the light suddenly sprawled over the ceiling

the interior was as drab and ordinary as its patrons

the furniture was lumpy, ornate and oak

his chambers consisted of a government-green room
trimmed in dark wood

a husky oak table

the unfinished elegance of a place where people are living slightly beyond their means

overstuffed chairs strewn with needlepoint pillows

the brocaded lounge

an antique with timeworn distinction

slightly frayed upholstery

the walls started to sweat

polished leather on a tufted couch

expensive decorative accessories that never called attention to their costliness

a mixture of warm leathers and bright prints

the main door had a fan over it like a halo

a splintered wooden stairway flecked with cobwebs

the room smelled of dust, mildew and old love

the single radiator clanked and hissed and constantly spit out steam and water

rancid grease hung in the air like a wet sheet

she felt dwarfed by the soaring pilasters and frescoed ceilings and gilt furniture

the curtains were frilly with a homemade look

the interior was cut down the center by a single corridor

blued fluorescent light

the mirrored wall was cluttered with . . .

clean, precise and exalting as a museum gallery

the room was almost spidery in its delicacy

the frenzied disorder proved marvelously comfortable

heavy steam, clouding the mirrors and sweating the tiles

Trade Tags

an indoor stone terrace with a ten-foot marble bar

a solarium with a tile floor and a trompe l'oeil ceiling

opulent, plaster-relief ceilings

a free-standing stairway of solid mahogany

a wall-to-wall river rock fireplace

complete with a wine-tasting room

with the most sophisticated security system available

the gracious solarium overlooks an English garden

a skylit artist studio

wedding cake chandeliers and rococo arches

elegant but understated furnishings

everything speaks softly of wealth and class

cedar-beamed cathedral ceilings and tile throughout

a dramatic twenty-foot-high entry foyer

perky cypress ceiling fans were in every room

a glass-walled card room overlooks the terrace

reveals an unerring sense of architectural composition

an entry of Italian marble and smoked glass

an ultrascience dine-in kitchen

a French attic bathroom flooded with natural light

CLOTHING

LADIES'—ALL TRADE TAGS

pencil-slim suit in jade and plum

a double-breasted smoking dress in red velvet

a Sherlock Holmes suit in brown wool

floating-scarf jacket in magenta wool velvet

cream-colored cashmere jumpsuit

olive suede pants

a cinnamon wool trench coat

a dapper cape-coat in putty gray

a cardinal red savannah shirt

cotton twill shirtdress in burnished gold

striped cotton T-dress in saddle and white

cochineal gauze dress

opal white drop-torso dress

a cotton watermelon-colored sweater dress

ecru canvas pants

aqua cotton cargo pants

white crinkled-silk cowled top

beige crop-top

shirred-hip skirt in powder blue

space-dyed jacquard sweater

peach cotton knit top

oyster white net vest

rubescent sweater vest

heathered beige and white dress

abstract-pattern cotton sweater

a velvet cocoon, bordered in fur

turquoise cotton chemise

a chocolate-colored duster coat

khaki pigsuede shorts

natural linen safari jacket

pre-washed red denim dress

peach crinkle-cotton pants

desert-green cotton jumpsuit

a cool spring shade of chambray linen

the palest pink cotton organdy

a full-backed linen tweed suit

red wool gabardine suit

white-striped silk crepe blouse

striped cotton-knit shirt

gray-and-white cotton mattress-ticking skirt

a spirited red shirtdress

black-and-white silk reverse tweed

black wool gabardine jacket

a pale yellow printed silk chiffon

a melange of plaids

a deep pink heavy silk crepe

peach linen jacket

ivory linen short pants

mink-colored easy jacket

peach silk handknit sweater

ivory linen lean skirt

sand linen handknit pull-on

blue cotton sheeting jumpsuit

burlap linen skirt

a natural silk sweater

ivory-and-blue striped silk shirt

floral-printed cotton broadcloth

charcoal gray linen with violet stripes

embroidered white cotton organdy

gray satin-weave linen

a sailor dress in cream-and-blue-striped wool

a pencil-thin black satin tunic

faded-blue cotton trousers

blazer trimmed in blue leather

white cotton voile

rich royal blue knits

a slim skirt in stone wool and angora

trousers of black cotton ottoman

a subtle jacquard stripe

a nostalgic tea dress in pale yellow

pink silk-crepe morocain tea dress

white linen blazer

black-and-cream silk crepe de chine

clam diggers in yellow and navy cotton poplin

a black cotton-lace dress

beige jacket of dobby-woven jute and cotton

a one-piece tracksuit in gray cotton melton

a chocolate scarf

an easy skirt in ginger wool jersey

satin-rich peau de soie

acid-yellow raincoat

a cocktail chemise in silk charmeuse

a fringed silk evening sweater

polka dot skirt in silk charmeuse jacquard

checked bourette silk coat

smocklike chemise in fuchsia cotton poplin

chemise in red floral-print silk

tomato wool jersey

nutmeg smock over a pink skirt

mustard brown tunic over a maroon shirt

inky blue linen

trouser suit in camel rayon

fawny beige wool coat

ivory lamb's wool and angora

black leather skirt

a color-happy floral print

long yellow linen tunic

classic black-and-white shantung suit

off-white suit of wool gabardine

a fire-engine-red cotton knit

a white cotton lanky knit tunic

long skirt of black silk crepon

African mud-cloth belt

a burnt orange calfskin bag

mustard whipsnake belt

lace-frosted silk peignoir

a butter-soft cashmere robe

a floaty peignoir shimmering with tiny pearls

ostrich feather jacket

an ecru satin gown with crystal beaded trim

a spy coat in brown wool melton

ivory-and-taupe wool velvet coat

low-flaring skirt in taupe cashmere

green jersey dress

white blouse over black turtleneck

a trapeze-top suit in cobalt blue

maroon nubby tweed jacket

a quince loafer jacket

pleated-back coat in saffron and amber tweed

two-toned swirl coat in russet and nut brown

a sophisticated suit in striped mauve wool

hip-hugging jacket in green napa leather

slim skirt in gunmetal leather

a pants suit in sooty gray

tailored coat in black and moss-green tweed

indigo print cotton dress

pearl linen suit

the "soft" suit, in coral linen

MEN'S—ALL TRADE TAGS

a ribbed and cable-trimmed vest

tartan plaid seersucker trousers

a cashmere cardigan in mint green

off-white corduroy pull-on pants

a seafarer sweater patterned with clipper ships

a cream-colored sandpiper sweater

a pullover with broad green and blue chest stripes

stonewashed cotton twill trousers

bird's-eye flecked cotton sweater in red and white

a cotton T-body sweater

unbleached cotton canvas slacks

waterproof skid-resistant boat shoes

cotton knit candy-striped polo shirt in cobalt and white

English bridle leather belt

imported espadrilles with jute soles

a jade smooth-knit polo

gray fleece-lined sweats

cotton jersey crewneck

warm onyx pullover with kangaroo pocket

sturdy cotton rugby shorts

terry-lined jacket with a signal flag design

gaudy awning-striped shirt

lavender pencil-striped shirt with a band collar

cool Madras pullover shirt

Oxford cloth over-the-head shirt

British twill walking shorts

windowpane plaid Oxford shirt

a bold-colored grosgrain ribbon belt

white tennis polo shirt

beige sueded-pigskin sportcoat

suede Tyrol hat with feather plume

supple cowhide leather trench coat

a deep brown grained-leather flight jacket

a Persian lamb ambassador hat

bomber jacket lined with sheepskin fleece

burgundy cowhide biker's jacket

black heavyweight cycle jacket

desert tan split-hide rancher's jacket

a bathrobe in burgundy wool tweed

a sand-pale cowboy hat

a long robe in a carnival-awning pattern

porridge-colored overcoat

vaguely military, vaguely Western clothes

a vester suit in striped wool

a Prince of Wales linen jacket

a loosely folded maroon pocket square

paisley tuxedo jacket with traditional center vent and notched lapels

cotton seersucker suit with narrow gray stripes

handsome navy blazer with brass buttons

a button-down Oxford dress shirt

hand-sewn leather loafers

traditional men's golf jacket

classic British tan trench coat

bright plaid pointed-collar shirt

kimono-style robe with patch pockets

a visored baseball cap

bar-stripe silk repp tie

classic silk foulard tie

embroidered pindot tie

typical olive-colored work pants

tan cotton-canvas workshirt

worn-looking stonewashed denims

burgundy boatneck shirt

zip jacket with drawstring hood

sweat pants with elasticized ankles

pull-on shorts with vented sides

bold-colored Hawaiian swim shorts

VARIED CLOTHING STYLES

too-short pants flapped like flags

rain removed the last memory of a crease from his trousers

the rather gaudy dresses of a woman past her prime

a hand heavy with rings

dressed in a wool coat and scarf against the autumn weather

wearing barbaric jewelry designed by no-talent friends

dressed with desperate respectability to inspire confidence

the belly-pouch of a gray sweat shirt

the wet shift was molded against her like a second skin

everything she wore fitted snugly

she believed in a brassy approach to fashion

sexy hip-wrapped minidress

she dressed like an extravagant shop window

a fluorescently clad group of men

dressed in forever-English stodginess

preferring eye-popping floral prints

a silken gown like silvery tissue

a collection of silver rings covered her fingers

a typical trench coated newscaster

her ring-cluttered hand

the dress was so heavily encrusted with rhinestones, it could have stood alone

an off-the-shoulder cocktail dress that dripped with sequins

ugly cloth coat fastened in front with wooden toggles

nothing fitted

his shoes were soft, comfortable kangaroo leather with high-laced cuffs that came up over his ankles

he wore gray denim trousers tucked into leather boots

he was wearing a denim suit (Oh, God, a denim suit!)

clad in a sofa chintz shirt

wearing an outré outfit

a born-again Christian Dior

dressed in Italian racing silks

wearing body fatigues

got the door open with a piece of flexible plastic

a man doesn't become an investigator without a capacity for cruelty

struck him with the flat of his hand, short, vicious, hard

the knife was all blade and alive

the edges of the knife writhed under his clothing

his fists struck invisibly, like the mouths of snakes

a man who didn't think but let his sinews rumble him to oblivion

his first foray into thrilldom

a wicked hawk-billed linoleum knife

and then came a moment of atavistic horror

carrying various impedimenta of murder

when he closed his hand around the knife, it completed him and made him whole

it was odds on that he'd been murdered

walks with a .357 Magnum on one hip and a .44 Bulldog revolver on the other

mentioned for his deeds of derring-do in strikes, etc.

are you under detention? arrest?

he waved his finger past his throat

the shouted orders, the slam-slam of heavy ammunition

the broken surfaces of his teeth shrieked

the angle of the sloped rifles neared synchronized perfection

violence-as-usual policy

his head erupted in blinding white pain

the unmistakable cluck of a hammer being cocked

machine guns made a soft *thew-thew-thew* as the bullets spit outward

black-leather-jacket ilk

hyped-up on cocaine

trying to prove themselves on two wheels

vrooming on the motorcycle

pile-driving blow

a front snap-kick to the groin

rear hug hold

knife-edge hand strike

drew his hand back and struck out

he stiffened menacingly

he could feel his panic rising

colors exploded in his brain

a boot slammed into his stomach choking off his breath

a fleck of saliva at the corner of his mouth

he was covered with blood and vomit

the bloodlust was at fever pitch

the thrill of the chase in his nostrils

he smashed his fist into the man's jaw and felt the bones give

grabbed her arm and broke it over his knee

a shoulder throw sent him crashing into the . . .

slight twisting of lips

she gasped and kicked viciously

her nails ripped at the man's eyes

as he reeled away, shudders began to rack him

the pain in the testicles streaked up to his stomach

the velvet trap of easy living and hard drugs

she took a deep breath, released, then sprang into movement like a sprung bear trap

the code of the vendetta was absolute

walking the knife-edge of danger

he represented uniformed authority, the military machine

he carried a two-foot steel jimmy inside his boot

a strange, cold excitement filled his whole being

an animal instinct told him all was not well

there was a strange, nervous unease about him

a pool of blood, not yet congealed, bloomed from his head in a small puddle

the automatic rifle tucked hard into his hip

the life went out of him like a winking light

the kids were hazing the dog with their ropes

no gun racks in the pickup truck

crazy, full-throated shrieking

the euphoria of heroin

he felt cool and alert like a boxer in training

his body was hard and quick and dangerous

a casual acceptance of violence

he ran like unleashed hell

it was called unarmed combat

shadow slashing

the bearing of a man perpetually on the lookout for trouble

the quiet, oiled click of gun slides being retracted

he had a vested interest in chaos

a man who despised uniformed authority

bunker mentality

an urban combat zone

ten hair-raising, heart-pounding minutes of terror

my goal is to stay out of the morgue drawer

pounded him into the ground

Get out of my face!

her face ravaged

TRADE TAGS

a false free alarm system

an innovative locking system with remote control

built with compression-resistant hinges

safe, secure, code-approved

chemically strengthened glass

can resist prolonged physical attacks

computerized tracking systems designed for officers not operators

double-window guards

a custom-designed intrusion detection system

the only thing that gets through our screens is light, air and sound

A system that shows you what's happening and where. Instantly

Guard dogs. Strong, aggressive, fully trained

chain-link fences with galvanized-steel posts anchored in cement

a .357 Magnum should do it

we teach all the arts: karate, judo, tae kwon do, kung fu . . .

DEPRESSION

the game was lost, the lights were fading
in the twilight world of the half alive
bad luck stomped through their lives
life in the last lane
theatrically miserable
hoping the wind and the rain would take away the brooding
hurt
he looked vacant, spent, all emotions smoothed away
restless, seeking
an infinitely sorrowful spirit
allowing a lachrymose little sigh escape his lips
the atmosphere was morose: exactly to his taste
an inner loneliness remained with her
she sat down, feebly, wrecked
even her lips felt cold
fatigue oozed from every pore
her heart went down, it sank, almost literally
the sickening sensation of your life plunging downward
a rush of bitter remembrance

heaviness in her chest felt like a millstone

she felt as if whole sections of her body were missing, torn away

a harrowing headache pounded her forehead

the loneliness had become a hollow

looked at her with a kind of sardonic weariness

he stood in the middle of a burning lake of himself, unable to escape

a strangely depressed emotion

the darkness pressed down on them

slumped into morose musings

shoulders drooped, gait slow and unsteady

a crown of gloom

mourning her own death

she was beyond pain, she was simply hanging on to survival

the ache she felt over the people she lost never really left her

she felt a rock fall through her heart

a devouring gulf of despair

always she wore a mask of hopelessness

as the tears of reality fell

the dead-end of hopelessness

pain and loneliness walked with him in the dark

his only feeling was a heavy, sodden dullness

a life which daily negated all her dreams

the covers protected her from the loneliness

always reliving defeats

she paused in her search for busyness to . . .

her wistfulness was like a recurring pain

tears flew down my cheeks like rain

pain swayed through her mind

CITYSCAPES

a fishy piece of moon scuttled behind the rooftops

the city wore a perpetual sulk

the highway was a sheet of glazed ice

the lights made a slanting yellow glow on the snow

the sort of place where tour buses stop

the constant assault of acidic air and brine

the city was under a smutty darkness

the disfigurements of urbanization

the grime of the industrial revolution

the highway scars of the automobile age

the world's center for elegance

the lamps pushed at the gloom

the gray purlieu of a large city

as sad and gray as the city he lived in

the strobic play of headlights down the row of pines

the street lights cast an orange, shadowless glow

a town with a yawning peace

a dismal soul-stifling town

traffic signals splintering in liquid reflection beneath her feet

a pall of smoke trailed out

the sky, like the city, was a dense slab of lead

a neat garden cooled by romantic, bubbling fountains

dirty clouds scummed the sky

as trains chuffed out in their clouds of smoke and steam

the burnt oil breath of machinery

the bus shook to a stop

a DC9-50 growled off the runway

the car roared into the headlight glare

the city had engines in its blood

he heard a car go by in a long suck, like a riptide

thwacking collision

the helicopters wheeled like vultures over the kill

rust bloomed like a skin rash in great orange blotches

a tremendous, many-fingered swirl of dark smoke puffed up

a world of neon-coated sleaze

the town was a six-stool restaurant

Trade Tags

a city that thrives on its rough-edged traditions

a cultured town, despite its tough-guy image

the streets are filled with honking cars, curious sounds, and tantalizing smells

step into this area and you've entered another world

the sidewalks function as all-directions promenades

a striking panorama of wood and glass skyscrapers

the speed of its lifestyle is definitely fast lane

a city with a glamorous and exciting mystique

a promised land that beckons platoons of aspiring talent

a trend-setting place

an experience in constant energy

the single most desirable address in the city

floors paved in white travertine marble

strictly an executive-entertainment home

electronically controlled wrought-iron gates

a skillful blending of stone and rare woods

great rooms with massive moldings

it has an identity

a boldly modern skylit entry

statues and concrete benches and straight narrow walks

a metropolis of parks and skyscrapers against a backdrop of tree-covered peaks

a mixture of the quaint, the spectacular and the tacky

the old neighborhood wears a new face

a successful blending of the old and the new

LANDSCAPES

above the horizon rose a blurred and red-blood sun

dusk filled the hills with purple mist

the shadows looked like stalking gray cats

dust was the only movement

clouds of yellow dust drifted from under the cottonwoods

as stark and bleak as a battlefield

peering into the shaggy corridors of white surrounding them

night swooped over the village

the scenery passing by was particularly dreary

the gray bones of the trees were beginning to show

watching the dark come on

the lawn was dotted with clumps of wounded grass

like stars of water on leaves

the white mums frilled themselves in the warm sun

looking up into the sun-shot leaves

faint puffs of vapor hung over the sodden fields

a green prison wall of trees

cornfields in a cover of whispering gray chaff

of glory in the flower

the fresh lie of snow was puffy and clean on the sloping lawns

the moon hid her face nervously in the clouds

the countryside, pastoral, verdant, unblemished

a beautifully wooded section of high bluffs intersected by ravines

the time of half light

the wet leaves and detritus of winter

a hawk scrolled the hot updrafts, precise and mindless, a part of things

a cloud reached out and grappled with the moon for possession of the night

the sort of place that would make an astronaut feel at home

the countryside was a dusty southern green

the night dew and the dust made grime

the line where the light stopped and the dark began

the morning was dying

the moon seemed bent on hurrying from one dark cloud to another

quick-moving shadows of clouds skimmed over the empty landscape

sun bathed the area with dazzling light

the treetops stirred with the whisper of a warming breeze

moonlight brought a magic aura to the garden

the wind fled, whimpering across the fields

night drew down like a black cowl

the branch bobbed, raining snow on her head

the sun-shot leaves that arched the path

as perfect as a scene inside an Easter egg

morning sun that was bright and crystal on this clear winter day

a medley of spring flowers

it was full dark

the color of wet sidewalk

beyond the scrim of dark mist

the night is dusted ash orange

the electric orange of the summer night

a turquoise sky filled with gold radiance

the darkness pressed down on him

strange and haunting like leaves blown through a forest at evening

Trade Tags

gently sloping lawns open to an incredible river vista

patchworks of sugarcane stretch to the sea

embrace deep, unspoiled valleys

rushing streams lined with tropical vegetation

lush plants thrive along the waterfalls

where the air is filled with mist and music

a ride in a safe and sun-blessed boat

swim in the wind-whipped waters of the bay

the still-sacred ruins of a massive temple

a time capsule of American culture

where the grounds are a paradise green

a walk through the highlands empurpled with heather

overlooking fields of peace

huge oak trees mushroom above the rooftops

with a view of acres and acres of waving wheat

the distant foothills are cloaked in velvet

surrounded by fields of waving wheat

look across hills of shining gold buttercups

located amid a profusion of pink bougainvillea and yellow hibiscus

an exquisite view of the cascading waterfalls

a country feeling prevails throughout

unparalleled natural beauty

three hundred and sixty degrees of lush mountain vistas

artistically sculpted gardens

nestled among picture-perfect aspen and blue spruce

with a stunning backdrop of rugged cliffs

a magnificent seven-acre retreat

WATERSCAPES

a pillaring thunderhead in the west marched toward their ship

tidewater seeped into his footsteps

the sea rose up and snarled at them

the gray-green gloom of the ocean

dark green ocean with a froth of autumn's russet

the waves lifted to the stars

the rainbow sheen of oil on twilight waters

the blinding dazzle of the sun's path on the quiet sea

our shadows ahead of us were long in a slanted pattern against the damp sand blue water rippled gently toward the shoreline

sights and sounds of a stream, its banks, and an old mill

the two arms of a seawall

marching steel rods of rain pelted the bridge

the faint moaning of new ice on the river

at the edge of the water, the land ends

a miasmic mist

bright flows the river

rough sea winds that swept like lost souls

the moon was like a lacing of crystals on the black-velvet water

a whiff of pungent sea air

the wind filling our sails . . .

Trade Tags

a vast natural aquarium where forests sway to a natural rhythm

a strange underwater world where wonder is the tutor

a blue world of coral reefs and clear, warm seas

a shore where kids shovel, sunbathers bask, and Frisbees fly

a village of fishing-port architecture

a deep-green bay, isolated, serene, sanctified

massive black rocks roar up from the water's edge

a uniquely romantic house overhanging the harbor

a long expanse of bulkheaded frontage on the river

a wondrously intricate lacework of bays, islands and coves

long fingers of land stretch into the sea

inside passages thread the islands from bay to bay

the ancient splendor of untouched shores

a coast scattered with charming village ports

a place that beckons you to cross the ocean

drop everything, buy a boat, and sail off into the sunset

the ultimate in leisure waterfront living

a panoramic view of turquoise waters and snow-capped mountains

---

EYES

EXPRESSION

amusement still lurked in his eyes

dark eyes with a sort of reserve he couldn't place

saw something flickering far back in those eyes

wise little eyes, bright and bemused

her eyes like a stream of gold in the dark

eyes as clever as a terrier's

his eyes slightly stirred to anger

large, timid eyes

soft, dark watchful eyes that missed nothing

his deep eyes showed the sensitivity of a scholar

with a tinge of sadness in her eyes

Indian eyes

an odd mingling of wariness and amusement in his eyes

the eyes of a doe

the sensitive, inspired eye of the artist

excitement in his eye

there was always laughter in his eyes

the sun broke into her eyes

an invitation in the smoldering depths

---

his eyes strangely veiled

big, droopy eyes

a lazy laughter in his eyes

veiled, liquid eyes

the message in his eyes was starkly sexual

her eyes were mirror brilliant

vampy, heavy-lidded eyes and a slight one-sided smile

blank eyes which gave nothing away

eyes, which by the dint of pure stupid instinct, were fearless

hard, gelatin eyes

boar-hog eyes

protruding eyes shadowed by thick brows

eyes hooded, mouth pursed

with a blank animal eye

her eyes clouded with hazy sadness

his eyes encased in thick spectacles

eyes that blurred with perpetual indecision

a wounded look in her dark eyes

his eyes were hard and cruel and pitiless

eyes as indecipherable as water

shrewd little chips of quartz

his eyes were covered with a milky translucent film

his toneless stare could bring a nurse to tears

the eyes like black holes in the pale face

her eyes were the beautiful blue of a robin's eggs and had just as much expression

death-bright eyes

twitching mechanical eyes

bold, black eyes . . . defiant

the whites of the man's eyes flashed

his eyes were little blue chinks in a set face

watery eyes with absolutely no expression

her eyes almost disappeared in her taut, bony cheeks

his eyes were a vicious glint in the failing light

her eyes expressed more challenge than curiosity

his pale eyes said, concentrate, take care

eyes alight like a fire, somewhat like an arsonist's

there was a real flicker of interest in her brown eyes

her eyes wide with the half-laugh that comes with fear

a look of intense, clear light poured through her eyes

eyes large and fierce with pain

a blue flame of defiance in her eyes

the icy-blue eyes radiated hatred and torment

little lightning bolts of worry darted into her eyes

feline eyes, arched brows and matte-red lips

staring at me from way inside herself like an animal looking out from the brush

eyes electric looking

fixed her in a blue-eyed vise

MOVEMENT

her eyes leaving his face for the flutter of a moment

blowing smoke, he followed the trail with his eye

now those brown eyes were *really* flashing

all eyes began to watch with renewed interest

his eyes dilating with sudden ecstasy

a crystal glittered in the rims of her eyeglasses

his eyes squinted with amusement

his practiced masculine eye took in every detail

she did a long, slow slide with her eyes

creases angled in toward the corner of the eyes

the lids drew down over the ingenious eyes

his eyes were watering in the wind

she looked at him with something very fragile in her eyes

all eyes gravitated to the golden girl on the beach

he looked up, now, fully into her eyes

stood there, gazing into private space

he looked up, and their eyes met for the first time

her dark eyes moved into his, seeing nothing else

she swivels her blue eyes upward

a glaze seemed to come down over his swimming eyes

he lowered his lids so that he could see out but no one could see in

something had come up behind her eyes

that knowing look, that smirking wink, was worse than . . .

her eyes were wet with anger

she saw the snap of his eyes

their eyes met and caught and a compact was given and received

they looked into each other's eyes as if they saw something new and deeply serious

he simply stared, his eyes obsidian black

. . . when their eyes separated . . .

her eyes flared up, but she cooled it

brows knitted in a frown

eyes squinted in embarrassment

eyes narrowed in pain

he stared at her until she blushed

his eagle eye stared down his heavy nose

staring at her with deadly concentration

stared after him, astounded

swept his audience with a piercing glance

his eyes probing her very soul

fixing his penetrating gaze on the speaker

his granite eyes locked on . . .

he cut a look from the newspaper to the clock

he pinned her with a long, silent scrutiny

a long and interested search

looked her straight in the eye and gave her clean answers

his eyes sweeping over her slender figure

there was a flash, like light caught in water, when her gaze crossed his

she looked up, her eyes shining

COLOR

it was her eyes, pale blue with a splash of green

his eyes were a quick gray green

his clean blue eyes were deeply set under prominent brows

her most remarkable feature . . . luminous, slightly protuberant green eyes

blue eyes with thick, sooty lashes

her large blue eyes vivid and questioning

eyes like clear black glass

smoky-blue eyes that tilted catlike

there were liquid blue shadows in her eyes

blue flecked with gray

chipped emeralds

blue eyes hidden under thick, yellow brows

eyes the color of gun metal

dark eyebrows arching over winter-blue eyes

a faded dust blue

a pair of icy blue eyes radiated hatred and torment

deep-set jet black eyes

wild, exotic sapphire eyes

hazel eyes with golden rims

slightly protruding coffee-brown eyes

her gold-green eyes wide with astonishment

the rare beauty of violet eyes and . . .

half-closed jade green eyes

inquisitive raisin-brown eyes

impatient brown eyes

the eyes swept with violet

fox-colored eyes

little turtle brown eyes

TRADE TAGS

brush on brilliance

express yourself with serious eye makeup

time of your life shades that are totally wow!

choose and fuse the colors together

the perfect solution for "allergy" eyes

the busiest little eye creme in the world

a new concept in custom-designed eyes

shades in four kicky colors

a chilling way to reduce eye puffiness is . . .

not specs, spectaculars

Puffy eyes? Help is in sight

the sophistication of silky lashes can be yours . . .

get the red out

she sat back, stung

his laughter stopped, as though he'd turned a valve in his chest

why not? he asked, getting excited

he was running on all eight cylinders now

whole streetloads of jubilation

feeling aggressive and alive, up on his toes

full of anticipatory adrenaline

she spent the next day in a state of controlled excitement

suddenly her blood rose in a jet

even the air seemed to be holding its breath

there was a vivacity, an air of enjoying life, about her

the way he moved carried its own excitement

an odd, volatile feeling about the whole country

he strode out of the house, raring to go

an increase in heartbeat, rate of respiration

they both rose: blood pressure and surface body temperature

she felt an electric sparkle, like knowing you're soon to go on holiday

she burst out, shocked

she took a quick breath of utter astonishment

wholly taken aback

it is totally beyond my ken to imagine that . . .

his mind kept trying to say things to his body

she felt that holiday tingle

a great exultation filled his chest to bursting

it was sheer naked drama

they nearly exploded with anticipation

a chill shock

with a whistle of surprise

the thrill of competition gave her vitality

a lot of bustle and brouhaha

total incredulity

though it hinted at danger, it had exciting implications

he felt a curious, tingling shock

he hated describing excitement instead of sharing it

they blinked in astonished silence

a strange, cold excitement filled his whole being

she felt a bursting of magic bubbles in her head

she realized with numb astonishment

she was the shock of life

with a look that made her breath leave her body

the party was a madness of glitter and glasses

her announcement was unexpected and shocking, but amusing

he was an endless surprise

uttered an indrawn gasp

surprised and somewhat thrilled by his own behavior

the grandness of his ambitions staggers me

DESCRIPTIONS

the upper-echelon mafioso type

his sunglasses veiled the contempt in his eyes

his face serious, dedicated

a thin, carefully clipped mustache

his face red from the cold

a long, narrow brown face, deeply seamed

an American Gothic face

his mustache looked as if it had been marked by a felt tip pen

the planes of his face were angular

his nose looked like a wedge of cheddar

pronounced cheekbones and sharp, clear chin

his face was granite, like his eyes

a square wall of a forehead with heavy brows for a base

a pale-complexioned, strong-profiled Englishwoman

his troubled face was like a graveled parking lot

a film of sweat on his face

perspiration on her forehead, like water beads on good butter the vein in his forehead swelled like a thick, black snake

his hawklike features arresting and elegant

a nose that could slice cheese

the face was long and bony . . . Dutch or Nordic at least

full lips set in a perpetual sneer

arrogant, sallow features

his dark, hawkish face seemed never to have known a smile

a shadowy ironic sneer hovered about his heavy mouth

her face was clear, almost bloodless

a haughty man with craggy features

a grayish pallor under his skin

a cigarette in one side of his mouth, the smoke sneering across his face

a drinker's veined face

he looked something like a hawk with mumps

her face was firmly set in deep thought

an obstinate mouth, an obstinate man

beads of perspiration sat at her temple

lips like a thread of scarlet

a gorgeous battlefield of wrinkles

a camellia-like complexion

a long, drooping mustached face

a sensuous face, direct and challenging

a sensual underlip

a fallen ringlet threw her brow in shadow

her prettiness was utterly commonplace

a kind of durably boyish face

like a face painted on a banner

high strong bones and large eyes

heavy boned and rakishly good looking

the sun caught her glasses, sending flares of light across her
face

face was coffin-shaped and elegant

elliptic nostrils

he had that kind of face, that kind of sincerity

his features were as handsomely sculpted as her own

her nose was slender and fine and the nostrils delicate

his full lips blended into a strong chin

high cheekbones accentuated her country-green eyes

a quiet, oval face, dark and rather delicate

classically handsome features

his nose was long and fine

high cheekbones, slightly arched nose

the clean purity of her profile

bruised grape-pulp lips

his crooked nose gave him a kind of rugged geniality

he had a face like a benediction

a ridge at the bridge of his nose where his glasses had
trenched

EXPRESSIONS

his homely face rearranged itself into a grin

he always got up with the face of a bad night

her face showed a delicate dimension of sensitivity

an "aw, shucks" look on his face

pushing his bottom lip forward in thought

staring with a combination of defiance and stupidity

his smug expression revealed an air of conquest

he pressed his lips together as a sign of pique

his glasses gave him an intellectual, rather interesting look

went around with a face like a stone

she pinched her lower lip with her teeth

he gave her a keep-your-mouth-shut look

she drew her lips in a tight smile

his features twisted into a maddening leer

horrified expression of disapproval

lips pursed suspiciously

cheek muscles that stood out when he clenched his jaw

he pulled his mouth in at the corners

a look of disbelief, rage and frustration

he put on his blank-television stare so no one could read his mind

the man stared mindlessly over the stern of the boat

her expression was pained, as though she'd been wounded

a little wary, a little haunted

a slight squint of the eye, a sideways movement of the jaw

she gave him a quick, denying glance

her face distorted with anger

you could see his arteries throbbing in his neck

he deliberately exaggerated the pain in his face

her face, hard, cruel, and pitiless

a prim and forbidding expression

arching her brows into triangles

a slightly blurred face, the kind you can't remember

a bright look of eagerness mixed with a strong stamp of arrogance

her fine, silky eyebrows rose a trifle

his face had the withered look of an empty balloon

her face collapsed into a complex set of wrinkles

her face fell in disappointment

her lips drooped sensuously at each corner

an oblique, quick, half-shy look

her wise-family-friend look

his face was totally devoid of any sign of recognition

a look that was compassionate, troubled and still

he had an alert, weakly handsome face

the point of her tongue slowly moistened her underlip

her face was old, but a child still looked out from her eyes

his features carried a startling load of information

his beefy face hovering over her

in repose, she was almost ugly, but in animation, she was beautiful

his eyebrows rose in obvious pleasure

the sunshine broke across his face

she sucked her mouth into a rosette

he had a well-used face

the amber flames in his eyes, the dazzling smile

his wry smile was hidden under an umbrella of a mustache

a sun-whacked face that tended to pout

a startled-fawn expression

TRADE TAGS

the difference between looking good and looking great

easily masks little imperfections

for a flawless matte finish, whisk your face with . . .

it lets the natural texture of your skin shine through

It's shine-free. You can hardly tell it's there

a surgical procedure that encourages the regeneration of smoother skin

you can't stop the aging process but you *can* forestall it

plagued with dark, no-sleep circles?

give your skin a vacation from cosmetics and apply . . .

for the alive-after-five look

in just minutes you'll look smoother, dewier, younger

a new dimension in performance cosmetics

develop a rich, golden tan faster and keep it longer

glow with health instead of a burn

for serious tanning buffs . . .

she stood in pleased surprise

she was in a lushy, romantic mood

Enjoy!

that wonderful sense of going home

his easy laugh spoke well of him

a blush of pleasure rose to her cheeks

her laugh was more like a whinny

a few crocuses of hope poked through the surface

lately there was a lightening of his scowling mood

as content as field mice in a harvest bin

the strange drug of calm

with a sigh louder than the surf before him

he let out a long exhalation of relief

she felt her reserve thaw

they drove for thirty minutes in full, satisfying silence

a small but satisfying victory

it seemed like an invitation to shared happiness

she liked him for the humor that glinted behind his eyes

a chorus of drawn-out "ohs," then laughter and excited applause

the feeling of happiness rising wonderfully inside you

feeling gay and relaxed and invincible

wrapped in a warm bunting of his own feelings

a warm kernel of happiness occupied the center of her being

a thrill shivered through her senses

beer-commercial joviality

blissfully happy, fully alive

he was loving every minute of it

it seemed to her something wonderful, beyond her

there was an indescribable softening

thoroughly enjoying the danger-excitement

a feeling of glorious happiness sprang up in her heart

when I feel this delicious, I laugh at practically anything, sometimes nothing at all

a real hard, solid laugh

INCENTIVE AND MOTIVATION

ALL TRADE TAGS

how to survive and succeed

demand the advantage

there's no substitute for a competitive edge

the days of the sound-the-same, look-alike approach are over

maintain and build your share of the market

the traditional public-relations-oriented approach won't work today

a total understanding of your current status

provide a maximum return

increase the effectiveness

outmaneuver the competition by taking strategic steps

pinpoint your target

learn to communicate our special product advantages

take a dynamic offensive stand

creative productivity

dare to be unique

forget the conservative middle-of-the-road philosophy

simple but persuasive messages

team effort

present a highly persuasive merchandising package

increase your awareness level

develop ideas by interacting with fellow workers

the power of a singular vision

actively expand your basic selling needs

strengthen your capabilities

leaving more time for self-motivation

first you have to identify your goals

put your subconscious to work for you

capitalizing on workers' strengths

centralize your interests

mental obstacles are the only barriers to success

improve your people skills

zero in on the target

the door of opportunity is unbelievably wide

an opportunity society

discard old career patterns

success begins with a great idea

learn how to look for opportunities and be ready for them

stay in touch and you'll stay in business

the power of initiative

be the first to master new innovations

stay on the cutting edge of your career

learn new competitive skills

critical thinking makes better problem solvers

broader base of knowledge

enthusiasm, the most important commodity you have

not just sure, *solidly* sure

dump the doubts

a high level of positive sensibilities

ascertain the value of your audience level

break out of the lineup

tough head-to-head competition

a persuader extraordinaire

develop a game plan

seek out what's new and different

dare to dream of total success

make things happen—for the better

redirect tension and stress

turn your unproductive hours into time well spent

reshape circumstances

create an alternative course of action

take a lesson from the superachievers

don't follow, blaze your own trail

familiarize yourself with the new techniques for moving ahead the opportunities are all there waiting for you

a person is responsible for his own development

put yourself in a mind-set for positive action

learn to compete constructively

turn self-doubts into self-assurance

project positive expectancies

creative ways to relieve work-related stress

the boldest, clearest, most professional . . .

if you think you deserve it, ask for it

reshape your confidence

essential business relationships are the key to influence

develop interdependent relationships

create an information base

determine where to spend your immediate efforts

learn how to manage diversity

evaluate your performance and personal commitment

uncover key leverage points

unencumbered by decomposing traditions

keep on top of the hot issues

centralize advance concepts

a sleeker, more streamlined approach

looking at yourself in the light of a new age

quicker response time

back to the drawing board, like hell!

stereotypical

the winners never quit

we need leaders, not overtrained execs

expanding your range of skills

real business savvy

analyze it and solve it

get rid of the bean-counter syndrome

experience and proven ability

when a customer comes through the door, love him

top drawer quality image

integrating your part into the total system

everything you do for quality improves productivity

the importance of public perception

another marketing first

concentrate on the future

the essential quality of inner strength

inspirational impact

power hitter

crisp, logical thinking

it was the only solid reality in a shifting world

learning to distance himself from humiliation and pain

the grave danger of taking himself too seriously

they were not enemies, but too cautious to be friends

the patience of a Russian peasant . . . and the deviousness

the rueful acceptance of a terrible knowledge

time is the wind that blows down the corridors, slamming all the doors

like a forgotten bead from a broken string

he took the world by the nose

you could catch it and kill it and pin it down, but then it wasn't a butterfly anymore

you can't fall off the floor

everything's copacetic

I still believe happiness can be worked out. I am a fool

against stupidity, even the gods contend in vain

by sensible, I mean with a touch of cowardice

there's nothing worse than a hero out of work

he was a bull and this was his grassland

people who censor books usually are illiterate

Christ, you didn't have to sling it all in the fan, did you?

The word was jungle. Only the strong survived

love was a weed that flourished in the dark

caught in the web of my own weaving

All's fair in love and war. Ask any divorce lawyer

it was the most beautiful experience of his life

a sense of place

Bastard! she whispered behind his back

listened with a vague sense of unreality

he found all his emotions agreeable

preoccupied with matters of nomenclature

she put her book down, but her eyes still rested on the afterimage of the text

regaining her shattered confidence

the idea slowly germinated within her

even now he felt ambivalent

she loved to snub him and enlighten him at the same time

yet deep, deep inside, he still burned with his love for her

she had secret threads of communication with other people

the contemplation of it would be anathema

she was rehearsed

when you have no blood relative in the world, you feel as if you're starting to disappear

she realized how carefully the old woman was estimating her

he felt cheaper than tattoos

it was as if a stone had dissolved inside her

her mind was a scalpel of reality

the fantasies that made her life bearable

there, just around the corners of her mind

her mind was narrow, repetitive and vapid

her dreams were attacked by common sense

the hunger to leave gnawed in his heart

her mind was always lost in the swimming future

he stared past the fire into his own thoughts

suddenly his mind blew open

it stood in front of the morning, that thought, killing all joy

her feminine perception operated instantly

no nonsense there, she thought

she looked away to the east, but he was part of the sky

he was locked into her mind

her senses still reached out into the night

tormented her mind

unstrung, at loose emotional ends

she knew with pulse-pounding certainty

a stab of feeling, a message across the darkness

suddenly, in a breathless instant of release, she was freed

the whole strange dreamlike lunacy of it all

her thoughts were like gliding clouds, fading in and out of the heavens

like the beginning of a new identity

it was like recognizing oneself

one of those short bouts of disconnected thoughts

her mind blocked the words of her consciousness

it was an intriguing, unsettling thought

he felt a ringing impulse of hope

entertaining the fantasy of . . .

oh, hell, she thought crankily

she'd been conscious only of cessation, of an emptiness that wasn't even loneliness

it dulled the cutting edge of her loneliness

to get away from everything was tempting

I think I know this guy . . . some guy

she must sort out her thoughts, arrange them, impose order

the thought whipped in so quickly that . . .

She listened and believed him. He believed himself

mechanically she went over and over the scene

hard work, thinking

with a dazzling leap of logic

searching anxiously for the meaning behind the words

he seemed to have tracked her thoughts

his thoughts whirred and lagged

sifting through it in his half-cosmic scholar's way

he was locked in her mind

trying to forecast the probable moves

finally, he began to resurface

melodramas filled his head

as though mesmerized by some marvelous ballet taking place in her head

with a lace of confused, pleasant thoughts

getting ready for the day's monotony

my mind just hung out a "Do Not Disturb" sign

she went back into her mind, into central control, and reset the relays

a quiet voice nudged her out of her musings

the years of terror were still locked deep inside her

if they couldn't get past this, they didn't have a future

during my youth, this was the string I plucked

a sense that things have spun out of control

I feel so unlovable, beyond the pale

of course he was sublimating his own misery

I have needed the illusion that I could still be useful

comforting, like a rune, something to hold on to

her life seemed to be drowning in overpowering circumstances

she could control her thoughts in any situation

it had been a frustrating and unique experience for him

a curious form of double-think

he had one sudden, cold, lucid thought

his hate was a living thing

his beeper held him on an electronic leash

for some shapeless reason, he thought . . .

his thoughts were fiercely concentrated

he chewed and thought and frowned

as bad as being told God dislikes you

all the pain resurfaced as she realized . . .

ADMIRABLE

as American as fast food

he had the organizational genius of a field marshal

a lot of control and a competent way of handling himself

rich, successful, tough-minded man who enjoyed the comfortable life

clear-headed enough to stop and stand still and look around

alive with prodded activity

it was easy for the minister to utter platitudes and false comforts

he was aware only of power, his power

big-game player

with the manner of the Grand Seigneur

braggadocio and macho bearing

a fire eater. Iron willed and hard as nails

the Colonel in him thought of the . . .

he could have easily played the role of an English tank commander in a war film

a brilliant strategist

there was a psychic link between the two women

the quality of animal assurance

they were the paragons of upper society

a young girl with mercurial quickness

she was quiet and deep but with an inbred force that . . .

behind that façade was an encyclopedic mind, a dynamic force

she had wit, directness and intelligence

a nervous, ambitious and energetic man

her rich English accent was saucy and provocative

a toasty-warm human being

of a more sensible, practical nature

daring and innovative

he never, but never, changed his mind

I was that "friend in high places"

it comes of being born and bred among the Mafia

with the utter frankness of the firm and practiced hunter

he had a masculine force about him, a great presence born of certainty

he was a dynastic man

obsessively devoted individual

always bearing what part of the burden she could

as a businessman, he was bold and controversial

they were the linchpin in the system

she was impeccable, impressive and likable

a man who had fought for everything he's ever gotten

she had a fierce, protective way about her

the canniest politician in Chicago

a person who would heal his own wounds

she generated awe

she had refreshingly ingenious warmth

with his combined roles, he held an awesome conglomerate of power

she was a luxury-loving lioness

he possessed sheer organizational muscle

sinuous brilliance, honed by years of training

impulsively dynamic

monumentally self-confident

with the temperament of an underfed grizzly

a woman who was more nanny than daredevil

he had a striking exotic quality people were attracted to

she's quite enigmatic, a cipher, really

he had drive and temper and shrewd intuitions

he wasn't menacing, but he was very sure of himself

he had the power of not being out of place himself, but of making everything around him seem shabby

like a long-distance runner just hitting his stride

the confidence of a healthy young man who has never been hurt

had the confidence level of a lion

the royal and the powerful

with the demeanor of a very capable head nurse

with the practiced eye of a man who made his living on
quick estimates

an Edith Wharton character who had everything she wanted

he was neutral in nothing

young, aggressive, pushing

a reed in his wife's storm

he had political talent, natural charm and the gift of
persuasion

he associated her with firm background, firm social place,
servants

a vividly inventive mind

a colloquial command of eight languages

as confident as one who has come into money

she had a quiet air of authority, and yet of rare warmth

the nimble brain of the entrepreneur

sure of himself and his easy power over women

the typical iron-core patriarch

with an engineer's rigidity, control and ordered mentality

an incredible energy behind his skills

a strong dauntless air about him

he was not a man who accepted second best in anything

a strong woman who could only be happy in a competitive
situation

the sort of man who started revolutions

a large and totally unpredictable bear

a staggeringly successful and accomplished man

the typical American success type

he could lose himself in a crowd of two

amiable, but intimidating

a genuine uptick in sensibility

with disarming friendliness

polite and tactfully incurious

her beauty and her sexual agility made all men her slaves

a wonderfully romantic, extravagant woman

a delicate yet provocative sensuousness about her

a built-in sense of social grace

a genteel, upper-class woman with no money

what a charmer he could be

she was warm-hearted, sensible and shockable

a young girl, totally at ease with her generation

his outward charm and openness masked a private man

Did she detect a grain of softness in that granite strength?

most optimistic Italian since Columbus

he was still capable of being shocked

a matinee idol of the old school

there was a lust for life about her

she had a touch-me look about her

top-drawer status

she had the calm visage of Queen Elizabeth in Essex

his style is easy and collegial

utterly likable and utterly competent

a costrategist

highly visible figure among the elite

a shrewd political strategist

you fill the room with light

straight talk and simple answers

a social lion

unerringly correct

his words had bite

she had a passion for unabashed opulence

WEAK

she walked in her proud humility, living within herself

a born whiner, all she asked for was a little neglect

over the years he had acquired skills, but not wisdom

a pathetically conformist way of life

obeying movements that had become a ritual

as complacent as a halibut

sitting quiet and humble even in her own house

all you get when you talk to him is a reflection of your own mind

his only saving grace was his wit

he was laid-back, never came on strong

a ditsy salesclerk

accustomed to her previous condition of servitude

there was a lack of immediacy about him

obviously handpicked for slowness

a woman grown old beyond the distance of understanding

a generous-hearted but rather limited man

a woman, but still pathetically girlish in behavior

a plain, dim-witted woman

they were beaten people, at the end of the line

she's hard, but she's not strong

he had other blind spots

she had no values, no dedications beyond her own walls

she did nothing that was not approved and conventional

lack of commitment and integrity

a precarious self-esteem

the women were paralyzed with respect and enchantment

he was a man she could mother and dominate

he fitted seamlessly into her life

a decent man in the wrong job

a man who neither forgot nor forgave

preferring his own world, secure like a walled mansion

there was a bitter pride there, like a lame boy who resents help

gentle and kind and stealthily insecure

a man who loved his wounds

self-punitive behavior

a born-to-worry nature

a man who craved the security of tradition

her little narrow convictions were firm and inflexible

work was her true God

he seemed dutiful, as if programmed to follow a course

he had the air of an outcast

a spiritless creature with a pale, unhealthy face

they were both not so much past their prime as having missed it altogether

a grim, gray, distant sort of person

a lavender hemlock

she had nothing to think about

she drew into herself to a spot inside no one could reach

another nobody

one day he'd tell them what he really thought

UNPLEASANT

he'd always been like a loaded dueling pistol with a hair-trigger temper

a violent man who enjoyed creating incidents in restaurants

with forced gaiety and theatrical bitchiness

he had a vested interest in chaos

she's a self-proclaimed watchtower of infidelity

became a wine snob and an art collector

acerbic woman who had a computer memory for . . .

one of those confident people who believes that, no matter what happens, he always knew it would

burned-out, haunted, cynical

a soul-deep flaw

little twerp

a nice, but not-quite-friend sort of person

more like a sexual voyeur

surly effeminacy

loathsome toad

soured with frustration

making her usual bitter, bitchy remarks

utterly charmless

no trip to Harvard . . .

little scanty people, meaningless and arrogant

the seismic fault of his life

about as animated as a robot in a sulk

with marine-corps sensitivity

a icy insolence

gallows humor

a hard-headed pragmatist

it was a classical sexist male-chauvinist put-down

a stiff, starched, bloodless individual

all in all, an intense, humorless individual

a truly poisonous little woman

the woman was a reincarnation of a killer shark

he picked people over like bric-a-brac

an air of jaded sullenness about him

he had no sense of humor

he outlasted better men through sheer insensitivity

there was a remoteness about him, like a barrier that no one could penetrate

witty, brittle playwright

coolly well-bred

the soul of a microchip

he exuded an odor of self-satisfaction

give him an inch and he thinks he's a ruler

sneeringly dismissed him

everything she did was rebellion

a small tear in the tent of grimness that enclosed him

OTHER

her highs and lows came and went with the weather, expected, but unpredictable

always restless for fresh horizons

a lively, turbulent person

a spur-of-the-moment man

he liked cool heads and turnip temperatures

a mild, vulnerable arrogance

she was more provocative than secretive

she seemed artificial, self-important

Control. He'd structured his life around that necessity

a stubborn perfectionist

she personified chaotic disorder

he's been middle-aged since birth

they had the same heavy, willing look

like a dog, peeing his boundaries into good order

as celibate as a monk

he leaves everything to hazard

she was the staple of daily conversation in the company lunchroom

she had an oblique way of informing them

a borderline intellectual

easygoing carelessness

her mental vocabulary was very limited

a hard-headed pragmatist

as if separated by a field of electronic force

his nature was cold and shrewd

a sallow and somber businessman

an aloof low-key sensuality

typically Victorian in her realistic assessment of facts

he conveyed his meaning clearly if not always gracefully

spending large amounts of money in the quiet manner of one who does it often

an arbiter of facts

a man without a past

empty posturing

her proud, honorable soul

she loathed sex

your idea of a vacation is coming back late from lunch

the big "gee whiz" type

you have a good career as a forger if you decide to go that way

a central-casting couple

not exactly raised in the embrace of high society

doesn't have both oars in the water

he was a nester, a homebody because he grew up humbly

he thinks gardening is living on the edge

a bunch of yahoos

a social caboose

the sunshade of my life

with war-zone ethics

a multiplicity of relationships is an avenue of growth

if for any reason, you feel the need to create trouble and pressure, then, by all means, do so

Why make little problems when you can create a holocaust?

be humble, but with an enormous, positive ego

if you have to discuss communication, you'll never have it

the conditioned mind anticipates

I live in a silent movie

your ball . . .

following the rules for the survival of the richest

a rough, school-yard element of justice

a fundamental appreciation of reality

going off the dole

a world of unchanging flux

she had the idea that one day he'd grow up and come back to her

the sheer logic of the idea was convincing

a coldly perfect world

a satisfying influx of Mexicans

the day you believe in your own publicity, it's all over

a woman's natural state is mysterious

not everything was cotton candy

they fitted together like rain and springtime

boys have a natural respect for consistency of behavior

like moving forever around an urn

she was desirable because she was so unreachable

a role befitting the ace forward on the basketball team

two nice people made for each other

by no means a world beater, but . . .

running against the current of academic tradition

seeking freedom from a crass civilization

the exhausted influence of her old mother

weighted by the pressures of conformity

the loose-lipped world of dealers

a person who has complete power over others becomes wicked

like an animal in a cage who, even if the door opened, wouldn't dare move

hope is one thing of which we are deprived

it's possessive to dislike reading a paper that has been passed through several hands

the ideas die away for lack of anything to hang them on

the wonderful thing about real conversation is that it stimulates one to new insights when you walk among women, do not forget your whip

character is formed in the world's torrent

conflict is a natural state of affairs

optimism is usually based on faulty logic

Who knows where terrific things begin?

he considered sloppiness a form of intuitive freedom

life is too good to be taken seriously

FEMALE

she was muscular, big, and bad tempered

a girl who had grown into a stupid, bovine woman

she was mirror brilliant and ice cold

a heavy peasant's body, sturdy and hard, bursting with juice

she stood five eleven and was at least a welterweight

with a rich, fawnlike beauty

her anthracite eyes and mop of blond hair

blissfully blond and deliriously dull

soft sag beneath the chin

her cool porcelain good looks

lavishly attractive

her long neck curved like a bird taking wing

she was attractive, special, sure of her power to please

her uniqueness was alluring

she was an unstylish, soft little woman

she was rosy cheeked, fresh, plump and tempting

with all the bloom of youth

a sizzling girl of summer

she was little and old and very nice

just enough lipstick to show that her mouth was perfect

windblown, sun glowing, salty, happy

looked the part of a pampered matron commonly displayed in society magazines

an arrogantly handsome woman of undisclosed age

a big, ripe-bodied blonde of about thirty

her stern was hefty, shapely, rich and unapproachable

a vividly beautiful woman

her bearing as subtle and sensuous as her mouth

a pouched and flabby neck

a small fluffy blonde, husky and pneumatic

her body was sensuous, sloe-eyed, half asleep

the long blond-haired cheerleader type

she was clean, tidy and unapproachable

she was tall, sensual, animal

a big mound of sternly coiffed beige hair

the sort one referred to as a "hill person"

narrow waist, wide hips and splendid wheels

sun-washed blond hair

a dusting of freckles on her cheeks

an incredibly desirable woman

a good hefty woman

sassily uptilted breasts

black, shrouded, plump and serious

pert, rounded breasts, remarkable in size

she was, simply put, a startlingly attractive woman

her hair, a tangerine pouf

shiny brown hair with Medusa-style locks

her hair flew out in silky tangles

her hair caught the light and was illuminated with wild drama

hair that had been teased with her fingers

her hair was simply washed and worn naturally

she wore her hair away from her face in a cleaned up hairdo

she wasn't tall, but she held herself like a queen

her skin smooth and sweet-smelling

as neatly packaged and self-contained as an egg

so fresh and excited that she gleamed

the slender but voluptuous body

her hips flared into long, straight thighs

an aura of untouchable glory about her

tall and formidable with a shiny smile that is the softest thing about her

cool and silvery and stainless

she was old, her legs withered, loose and blue-veined

there was something terribly plastic looking about her

her beauty was so unearthly it was frightening

great hair, wonderful legs, and a beautiful smile

her breasts were high and full

her nipples were erect from the cold

but from behind, she looked her age

her seductive young body and wholesome good looks

she looked like a goddamn Girl Guide

clearly revealed the gentle curve of her full buttocks

she was beautiful with the bounteous magnificence of an earth mother

her taut nipples strained against the thin fabric

an identical remake of her mother

like a black panther, darkly beautiful, but deadly

a long-stemmed, big-breasted woman

tall, slender, with careful elegant grooming

the cool grace of a hedonist

her hair framing her face and elongating her neck

sliver-thin eyebrows shaved at a permanent arch

her hair a perfect style for the richness of her clothes

a lovely, skillfully made, richly evocative woman

hair the color of warm honey

a tight face that was drained of color

her deep auburn hair shone bronze and gold in the sun

not exactly an exciting challenge

hair as stiff and black as raven's wings

thick black hair and button brown eyes

bouncing hair and shining eyes

hair falling uncurled down her back

hair that had grown coarse with bleach

her hair was a plume of black gold falling to her waist

full, dark hair, just graying at the temples

fine, curly, golden hair

dark red-gold hair that fell into indigo-blue eyes

light, wheat-colored hair glistening with golden streaks

a razor haircut, stiff with spray

her long auburn waves dazzling the sunlight

loose wisps of hair made dark commas on her neck

dark hair, prematurely flecked with gray

silver-blond hair worn straight and long

the silver swing of her hair

hair as black as Manchester coal

a beautiful china-skinned blond girl

MALE

he could throw a softball like a cannon shot

a course, insolent looking man with an obese money bag

muscular arms wedged into a black T-shirt

he was built like a beer wagon with two hands that would cover this table

muscles bulged and slid under the red-bronze tan

awesomely muscled

a tight-knot man with bottle green eyes

a hard jaw, tendoned neck, deep chest

a hammy forefinger

the glistening muscles, hard, distinct

a big, florid man

tall and rangy-rugged

his bulging muscles noticeably outlined the business suit

there was something awkward and milkfed about him, like a calf

his hands were damply flaccid and thick fingered

rounded shoulders, bent back, protruding potbelly

a vigorous, elfin man

his arms looked like they'd been squeezed from tubes

his arms seemed to be as boneless as tentacles

he was her flour-faced husband

a short, plump polyp of a man

he had the pallor of desk work

tall and straight, lithe and supple

an obese, balding, sloppy middle-aged man

a badly preserved forty-nine

he looked like the torpedo had already left the tube

remote, majestic figure in splendid boots

a tall distinguished-looking man in his late forties

on the tall side of six feet

slim but powerfully built

sword-thin

The man was exquisite. There was no other word for it

a built-for-action body

he arrived wearing jeans and his signature pout

his body was shaped like a thimble

as shriveled as an old orange

lithe as a snake

he was gray-white and toughened like a dry hide

a physical monument to the terminal quality of youth

he looked like a little wet bird

Mr. Body-perfect

whippet thinness

a tall, richly urbane gentleman

his appearance always infused new hope

a look of ingrained snobbery

a gangly youth with a blotchy face

good looks had been bred out

adjutant in appearance, tall, thin, mustached, swarthy

almost as tall as a flag pole

two dark types came in and sat beside him

though small and wiry, he looked larger, harder

instinctively on guard, like a pit bull in a ring

he stood tall and, yes, impressive

the fat, placid stereotype of a bartender

the fluid, rippling motion of the muscles in his back and shoulders

the years had chipped off like ice from a pipe

a high-yellow negro

his honey-colored skin glistened with sweat

tall, slim, suave, graying . . .

long-legged and slender and full of vibrant engines

like a fine-spun dancer, his body was slender but not sparse

thin as a wafer

a lumbering Sumo wrestler

callused hands, massive oarsman shoulders

rough black hair fell almost to his eyebrows

a nose the size and color of an apple

with ginger freckles on his bald skull

prominent patrician nose

a well-dressed man, never overdone or dramatic

he looked like a man who had found his grail

a tanned chest, covered with rows of gold chains

a lanky frame without one ounce of spare flesh

he always appeared bowed down with unutterable burdens

heavy-boned and rakishly good looking

a true geriatric miracle

with the meticulous grooming and self-satisfaction of a TV lawyer

languid, slimly muscled grace

an oak of a man

a white walrus mustache

each hair on his head lying obediently in place

whisk-broom beard

bear hair, thatch black and curling out of the throat of his shirt

his chest, a bed of curly hair

his hair was soot-gray and shaggy

bald, except for a monkish fringe of white hair

his hair grew upward and outward in great masses of curls

going bald in back

thick sandy hair and a red beard

a loose thatch of hair across his forehead

his slick locks combed sideways to conceal the tonsure

the white blond of an albino

red hair that spiked straight up

a wispy mustache that would never be anything but wispy

a shock of woolly blond hair that needed cutting

unmanageable hair was another persistent problem of his life

skin as dark and shiny as black chintz

grungy looking

a courtly Texan

a *Little House on the Prairie* hairstyle

a body as limp as filleted fish

pale face and subtle eyes

iron-brown eyebrows and powder-white hair

as thin as a nasal voice

TRADE TAGS

Innovation. We've been breeding it for thirty years

design-elevated to pare away all nonessentials

laying bare a whole new concept

take what you have and make it better

revel in the unexpected

tenacity and technology is what makes the difference

designed to make the most tasteful statement ever

for a head start in the future

truly individual, with telling custom touches

a classic with a dash of the unexpected

it will spoil you for everything else

designed to trigger actions, and reactions

more features, more options, more flexibility

it's got the power to astonish you

in the race for excellence, we dust the competition

sharpen your sensitivity with innovative . . .

a shared secret enjoyed since 1830

remarkable operational features, intricate detailing

a masterpiece of quality

unparalleled authenticity

hand assembled by dedicated craftsmen

tantalize your partner with the most provocative . . .

create more intimacy in your relationship

with head-turning breakthrough looks

designed to make you look good and feel naughty

authentically guaranteed by the distinctive

understated elegance

luxurious appointments

unbelievable attention to detail

uncompromised quiet

add pleasure, subtract expense

special moments happen everyday in . . .

so when only the finest will do, call . . .

be daring while you're being sensible

experience the world of shimmering silks and glittering gems

more capability than any other . . .

it's not just a tool, it's an inspiration

to complement this hushed and luscious environment

to feel totally enchanting

if you want romance to come on strong

for the ultimate in styling versatility

all around is a panoramic expanse of window area
allow us to pour on more pleasure
at a price you can afford to enjoy
Portable. Storable. Affordable.
Cool elegance. Refined sophistication
classics don't need hype, just women of impeccable taste
within this small box lies the promise of . . .
one of the finer things in life is finally affordable
don't simply imagine it, indulge in it
grab a little comfort with . . .
Don't pamper it, enjoy it.
a range of performance features
an awe-inspiring itinerary
incredibly soft and expandable
it's uniquely constructed frame can stand up to . . .
we've caught the competition sleeping again
new gracefully sculpted lines
its integral strength, its luxury, its easy handling
its technology is beautifully evident
spectacularly dramatic island coastline
sleek, smooth and aggressively dynamic
beneath its beautifully sculpted features
it handles the job with composed confidence
we've taken the concept of xxxx into a whole new
dimension

we're not only bigger, we're a giant

create a niche in your life for one perfect thing

we cater to your every whim with unmatched elegance

a pure delight in precious gold

Guaranteed. Period.

a fantastic shape and purely practical

the new essence of elegance

superbly created with love

designed with tailored, smooth-flowing lines

an eminently sensible . . .

its allure is as mysterious as it is personal

the elegant opulence of dazzling . . .

we remain small so we can concentrate on high-quality production

quality requires a certain character, a degree of perfection

sophistication with an erotic flair

shockingly lurid in detail

exaggerated sentimentality

the electrifying lure of brilliance

mind-blowing perfection

we have the indecency to be astonishingly candid about our . . .

with a captivating hint of ecstasy

the extraordinary treasures of the night are yours

it came from a family of winners

first-class is a way of life
with a blatantly sexy sheen
a silky little slip of color
made with extracts that pamper, protect and preserve
your hands will want to touch
for a pulse-quickening experience
again and again your eye will return to . . .
we've flaunted the standards of the past
portraying the very essence of life's beauty
uncompromising quality, purity and simplicity
our dream of perfection became a part of history
snub convention and indulge your whim
it's one breath-taking cliff-hanger
it's pure ostentatious glitz
big, strong, bulletlike
unmistakably masculine
featuring our new beefed-up . . .
the sleekest, hottest-looking item on the street
Bold. Taut. Masculine.
we deliver more power than the toughest
discernably smoother and cleaner than any other
as sensuously soft as satin
a design that flies in the face of convention
an exhilarating status symbol

Start by stirring emotions. Start with a . . .

quality construction, award-winning design, luxury accents

an opportunity afforded to only the discriminating

exquisite detail with every amenity imaginable

magnificent in design and execution

replenish the spirit with . . .

unleash the ultimate

rich, redolent, robust and gutsy

elegant styling with a special sensitivity to . . .

So rare. And available to so few.

a hybrid of the classic line of . . .

made with the same exacting standards as its original

unique quality for a privileged few

sophisticated, subtle, sexy

and for your ego, something that's absolutely perfect

delicacy is its strongest point

a light-catching finish

something to trigger your awareness

the origin of enchantment

a whole new color experience

how can something this exquisite perform so well?

awaken the temptress in you

experience the romantic sensation of . . .

racy, daring spaciousness

yield to the impulse

the new world luxury of revelation

designed to fire the imagination

inside its sleek interior is a . . .

practically perfect

satisfying the specialness of both sexes

don't just experience elegance, become a part of it

explore the intimate delights of . . .

nobody sets the stage like we do

the promise of unspoiled paradise

your experience begins the moment you come on board

offering both immediate enjoyment and long-term pleasure

a wealth of sumptuous appointments

if you want to shake up your life

it reeks of masculinity

make a beeline to your dealer

the world is full of utterly predictable gifts

totally emotional and thoroughly practical

there's virtually nothing we can't provide

feel positive again

a fusing of intelligence and imagination

gift wrap the gal in your life

inhale the cleanest, crispest air you've ever breathed

with one eye on the drawing board and the other on your needs

unsurpassed smoothness and unique character

unfortunately only a few will be able to enjoy . . .

it sparkles under pressure

It's your choice. You decide.

until recently you were forced to choose between

the grandeur, beauty and magic of . . .

redolently rich in flavor, texture, freshness, diversity

the result is a complex blend of . . .

the highest level of smoothness obtainable

a refinement to satisfy the aristocrats

we back what we build

because simpler things usually last longer

with an unheard-of ten year warranty

crisp, clear, uncomparably smooth

its natural beauty enriched by an aura of romance

dignified, breath-taking and obtainable

an evolution into creative daring

ours is the one others try to copy

classy design and snazzy multicolor paint

born with the expert touch of the craftsman's hands

experience the rare, the unforgettable, the sublime

a good excuse to take the long way home

expression of carefree innocence

designed to give you brilliant choices

stunningly bold

crafted to endure both time and trend

live an adventure of pure luxury

where gentle strength triumphs

it's not difficult to inject new notions when . . .

for the decorum conscious

a whole different philosophy of operation

outrageously delicious

for the uncompromising woman who can afford any address

it's the absolute Ritz of travel

with a high international profile

presented with grace, wit, and a sense of playfulness

a new destination in color

a place where timeless images endure

with an innovative new direction

let the winds of self-expression prevail

YOUNG ADULT TRADE TAGS

exciting, self-directed

no gluing, no cutting, no staples or tape

for great social and physical growth

when you're ready to attract attention . . .

do it in bubble-gum-pink racing shoes

in lots of fabulous fashion colors

here's the deal: send in ten labels . . .

for the fast-track girl

get ready for the big pitch

win 100s of neat prizes

for a whole new look

hide the nerves inside with . . .

your choice of gifts

in high-energy, high-intensity colors

get that winter glow

handsomely designed and made of authentic . . .

establish a pattern of excellence

it's built for fun

straight from Paris

in fifteen sizzling shades of . . .

a totally new and refreshing approach

express yourself with confidence

a dynamite collection of related separates

if you care about having healthier-looking skin . . .

whatever your mood, say it with . . .

for the look you'll feel good about

with a free . . .

QUESTIONS

the question hung between them, unasked, unanswered
she asked the air
his brows lifted a question
she slanted him a question
the question was hideous and alluring
a clumsily worded request
the question was a stab in the heart
What the hell?
Why? she quizzed herself silently
the unanswered questions hounded her sleep
a mocking voice inside insisted on answers
a cynical inner voice brought another question to mind
the quick question needed a thoughtful answer
another puzzling thought to worry about
Why couldn't she fit the pieces together?
she waited expectantly, but the question didn't come
it wasn't a question, it was an inquiry
How dare he interrogate her like that?

her mind bulged with unasked questions
What did he expect?
the question brought a hushed silence to the courtroom
the type who always answered a question with a question
God, now what?

REMEMBERING

in spite of his resolve, inexorably, his mind returned to . . .

going back, picking up the strings of time

the memory edged his teeth

a memory ruffled through her mind like wind on water

it had an emotional resonance that lingered

she remembered the aftermath, too

allowing the subconscious to surface

she double-checked her memory

her fragile soul couldn't bear the black memories that had scorched it once

opening the door on a lot of memories he'd tried to bury

the flood gates had opened and the torment was finding its way out

the thought made her throat ache with regret

he sank into the deep chair and was filled with remembering

he smiled with remembered pleasure

trying to recapture the dimly remembered gentility

slowly, he submerged himself into memory

she never alluded to what he had done

her brain combed out the tangles of the past

the word "picnic" has taken me on a long journey in the heartland

wondering if she had let an idyllic state slip by without savoring its sweetness

as she picked up the strings of time

memories, so vivid, so close

the memory was like a film rolling on

the picture was lost, no longer in focus

the memories came crowding back, like a hidden current

memories were searched and researched

remembering the adventurous anticipation of his youth

she remembered unwillingly

memory closed around her and filled her with a longing to turn back

her mind thumbed through all the names and faces she had learned

he huddled, protecting that place in his heart that only Mary had ever reached

she deliberately let her mind run backwards

he listened to some distant experience

a dim ripple ran across his mind

a black veil moving painfully at the back of his mind

in the journey of life he came to a dark wood

her mind floating in a sepia haze

flipping through his memory file

if she had ever loved him, she had forgotten it

spurred by the jockey of memory

back in another compartment of her head

her mind flipping through a mental atlas of faraway places

memories opened before him as if a curtain had been ripped aside

ATTRACTION, DESIRE

found him disturbingly attractive

his admiring gaze gratified her

gobbling her with his eyes

pleased at her open delight

he came on a little, but . . .

raked her with a fiercely possessive look

his eyes glinting with pure masculine interest

a man who was an exciting challenge

she watched his eyes grow hungry

fully aware of his rugged, masculine appeal

she could feel the power of his gaze

stunned by the intensity of his vibes

met his flinty gaze head-on

she was aware of the hunger in him

her femininity responding to his masculinity

interest radiated from the dark depths of his eyes

the magnetic pull of his masculinity

she was attracted to this daring, handsome stranger

eyeing her with a look of scorching intent

there was something she instinctively liked about him

shafts of electricity coursing through her veins

his gaze focusing on her lips

the sensation brought a warm tingle to her depths

he smiled when she glared at him

his look traveled up and down her

she could almost feel his thoughts

she studied him silently and the cool blue eyes studied her back

she was a little in awe of him, confused by his easy charm

a sense of tingling delight began to flow through her

though cynical and a shade wary, he had a languid charm

he was different, gentle but direct

she could feel across the room the surging power of his presence

an intense physical awareness of each other

he liked the textures, juices, spices of her

she was neither embarrassed nor distressed by her reactions

each sensing a reserve in the other

her heart reacted immediately to his gaze

he was more challenging than comforting

with a shuddering sigh, she watched him go

her heart thudded like a drum when she saw him

she liked him for the humor that glinted behind those eyes

his glance was lazily seductive

a strange and almost imperceptible tremor

she liked the curve of his mouth, the gentleness in his eyes, the graceful strength of his hands

never had she felt such an exhilarating response to any man

he looked at her with something deeper than mere masculine interest

a rush of feeling that was elemental and very alien

the psy-war between them was . . .

no longer adversaries, instinctively on guard

the tenuous link between them

he exuded a reckless passion

the woman inside of her started to come alive

she couldn't resist his potent brand of sensuality

excitement mounting within him

she was high on his list of objects of use and beauty

the prohibition on touching excited him

furious at her vulnerability to him

confused by her own rampageous reactions

she shivered imperceptively at the husky tone of his voice

caressing her with his eyes

she could feel his surging physical examination

she felt herself flowing toward him

his eyes met hers, filled with desire

he let his eyes roam over her figure

she flushed as a rush of warmth flashed over her

a response as age-old as the sea

she felt an immediate and total attraction

it had been a while since a man had noticed her; correction, since she had noticed a man

surrounded by an aura of irresistible femininity

they both seemed to be in the process of discovery

fuddled by longing

he enjoyed this kind of sweet warfare

blithely ignoring the voice of reason that said no

she said sweetly, still playing the game

his steely gray eyes shot her a covetous look

spellbound with sensations that were new and compelling

a feeling of streaming hope

trying to get his aggression under control

twice, now, men had come between her and her dreams

reality took second place to dreams

I wish I had her sail on my boat

she had just shared an important part of her life with him

her heart shuddered expectantly

they shared the same faults

dismayed when she came upon the unsuspecting shallows

even in the privacy of her own heart

it was a definite turn-on

his arresting good looks totally captivated her

she couldn't cope with someone who was naturally good

the torment of his presence

she could feel the giveaway heat in her face

she was more exciting than cuddly

his heart slammed into his ribs

an unexpected tremor of pure desire

a trembling thrill raced through her

straightening in a reflex response to his leashed power

somewhere between disbelief and enchantment

untethered desire

hungry for his touch but knowing she didn't deserve it

the sensuous flame of life

a strong and husky relationship

it sent another wave of warmth along her pulses

the main interest of his life was the pleasuring of women

sitting weakly in the electric silence between them

sparks of unwanted excitement shot through her

tremors of rapture caught in her throat

playing the game with purpose

a sensuous smile came to life on his lips

with an intensity, a masculine hunger that unnerved her

trying to still the wild pounding of her own heart

wrapped her in the warm bunting of his own feelings

she felt her heart skip again, and again

the staggering challenge of his nearness

she used her sexual attractiveness to get her own way

he took a look down her décolleté

he stood so close she could feel the heat from his body

fleeting thoughts of sleeping with him pranced through her head

he tried to look casual, but she could almost smell his excitement

struggling to tame the urge to take her

the dormant sexuality of her body had been awakened

the impulse to reach out and touch her was almost a tangible urge

a deadlock of passion between them

she could feel the angry warmth of his nearness

a jolt of desire forced her to look away

the heavy ache of male hunger

watched his sultry gaze rest briefly on her breasts

her need for him was more compelling than sexual fulfillment

it was a sensuous and persuasive feeling

she let herself fantasize about getting involved with him

carefully he pushed through her zone of untouchability

emphasizing the sway of her hips because she knew he was watching her common sense skittered into the shadows

even his name seemed carved into her heart

the fires within her shot upward and outward

as she dried herself, she realized how sexually aware of him
she'd become

learning each other's moods and flash points

she loved him with a queer mixture of contempt and desire

it had been awareness, invitation, acceptance, all in a few
moments

she had a wild urge to throw herself into his arms

TOUCHING

the touch of his hand ran up through her arm

draped an arm lightly about her shoulders

she felt crushed by his strength

handling her as if he owned her

lean masculine planes and hard-muscled ridges under her
fingers

all of the air expelled from his lungs in one wild gasp

she opened her arms and he came into them

she tried to protest, but her vocal chords stalled

if he had to use force to get her, that's what he'd do

he stood close, his body pressing into hers

his hands spanned her waist, drawing her to him

. . . the whisper of his breath on her cheek

the pressure of his hands, the firmness of his body

her senses began to flutter in response to his kiss

surrendering to the crush of feelings that drew them together

her response was shameless, instant and total

ragged whimpers of sheer need escaped her lips

wrapping both arms around her, he crushed her to him

she trembled in his arms

she was conscious only of his nearness, his lips

sending fire through every nerve in her body

steeling herself against the tide of pleasure that was threatening to carry her away

her body pressed against his sinuous limbs

he wanted to conquer her, not comfort her

her senses throbbing with the strength and feel and scent of him

surrendering to the crush of feelings that drew them together

a hands-on kind of person

what she had was hot and stimulating

her touch triggered primitive yearnings

leaning against his sinewy length for support

lifted her hands to his shoulders, clinging to him

the tingling effects of the contact spread through her like wildfire

relaxing, responding to the tender touch

he courted her senses with gentle persuasiveness

he pressed every inch of her body to his

his powerful body rippling with tension

a primitive act of domination

uneasy at the sudden physical intimacy

feeling the warmth of his hand on her shoulder

his touch sent shooting stars up her arm

wrapped her arms around his waist

feeling the drumbeat of his heart

expressing their feelings through loving gestures

his hand swept to the back of her neck

nestling against his supple strength

her own hunger came on in a heated gush

she pulled away, flustered by the extended contact

her hands skimming over the rough textures of his body

a light touch that unfurled streamers of sensations

drawing her against him until she was aware of his entire length

slapped her fondly on the buttocks

a hug which ended up with a firm pat on the fanny

a warm wave of breath in her ear

her finger traced the shadow of his lower lip

communicating her desire for him in a primitive fashion

caught up in the pleasure pulsing through her

KISSES

his lips brushed hers, a tantalizing invitation for more

trailing a path along the side of her cheek with his tongue

his mouth warm and demanding

he smiled against her mouth

when he bent his head, she met his lips half-way

when he tried to kiss her, he got a cheek and a slow move back

he kissed her in the moist hollow of her throat

whisper-light contact of their lips

a wild, hungry caress

bending down, he lightly pressed his lips to hers

his lips blazed a trail of liquid fire across her smooth skin

his mouth wandered up the tingling cord of her neck

she embraced him and kissed his cheek, her arms solid and strong around him

his lips touched hers, featherlike

breathless and urgent

moving against him in a suggestive body caress

a kiss full of passion and need

her mouth was smothered by his warm lips

the sweet throbbing of his lips made her shift closer to him

a small sound of wonder came from her throat

his mouth moved over hers in a sensuous exploration

his lips were surprisingly soft and sensitive as they rested on her own

he took her lips in a soft, moist kiss

his head lowered, his mouth met hers

his rough, aggressive kiss held her captive

his mouth claimed hers in savage conquest

it was a light, questing kiss

with a soft sigh, he settled his mouth on hers

he planted taunting little kisses along her cheek

his kiss was easy, practiced . . .

he lifted his lips until they hovered just above hers

his kiss was overpowering and passionless

the wildly masculine sensation of his kiss

his lips seized hers in a deep emotional commitment

a perfunctory kiss that stung more than a slap would have

he insisted that she answer his kiss

the breathless wonder of that first kiss

he kissed with a punishing sweetness

it was a light kiss but a tender, lingering one

his lips met hers in a gentle drugging kiss

his mouth moved over hers with exquisite tenderness

his mouth massaged hers with provocative insistence

parting her lips, she let him possess her mouth

with a lazy, sensuous movement, his tongue entered her mouth languidly, his tongue entwined with hers

a deep, achingly sweet exploration of her mouth

nothing could have prepared her for the explosion of his kiss

a wild surge of pleasure as his mouth opened over hers

his tongue swept inside to caress the walls of her mouth

his thrusting tongue pushed her toward new sensations

his tongue met the smooth wetness of her teeth

their tongues sought each other's out

his tongue moved into her mouth with urgent passion

he had to slide his lips to one side to get a breath

parting her lips in mute invitation

her lips opened to him

his tongue stabbed at her lips

he used his teeth to force her mouth open

while he explored her mouth, she tasted him with a new hunger

there was passion in his kiss, but also anger

her lips opened fully, like a morning glory

then slowly the pressure of his lips increased

their tongues danced together in a silent melody

she opened her mouth with a small whimper

moving his tongue over hers with rough thrusts

his lips were like velvet as his tongue explored . . .

. . . and then he *really* kissed her

nudging his tongue against her lips

painting the roof of her mouth with his tongue

his tongue moved inside her with strong, impelling strokes

his hot tongue caressed the inner walls of her mouth

his kiss white-hot

the moistness of her open mouth

familiarizing himself with the dark velvet recesses of her mouth

his tongue ravaged the sweetness of her mouth

she clung to him, wanting the kiss to go on

pulling away with a tearing reluctance

wishing the kiss would last forever

LOVEMAKING

strong and vivid desires coursed through her

his fingers fumbled with the buttons of his sweater

as she pressed against him she could feel his impatience

brushing her fingers across the dark curling hair of his chest

the steadily tightening coil in his lower regions

trying to get her to relax with him

wanting to unleash his hunger and satisfy it

caressing him gently with loving fingertips

a mutual shudder ran along their length

feeling the raw warmth of his skin beneath her fingertips

her body glowed warm and welcoming

he moved against her, fanning the sparks of arousal into a leaping flame

her lips flickered over his skin with hot desire

surging physical excitement

trembling against his warm, virile nearness

her body burning his flesh

she found a new and passionate woman inside of her

her desire was primitive . . . exciting

their hands feathered over each other's bodies

her body, alive now, yearned for a conqueror

she felt the thundering of his heart pounding against her breasts

her softness moved against his caresses

his naked chest melded to hers

burying himself in her softness

the enchantingly smooth textures of her body

sex is acceptable exercise

sex tones the body and makes two people feel good

he pressed her belly hard against his

trying to still the twisting desire in his loins

a gentle moan of passion escaped her lips

swept away by waves of new experiences

surrendering to her overheated senses

stretching out beside him with loose-limbed grace

what she had was hot and stimulating

his arousal already beyond the point of control

his knowledge of sexual arts was prodigious

caressing her body with his tongue

exuding a sensuality and a heat that . . .

her breasts thrust toward him, firm and full

glorying in the feel of her silken flesh

she felt her body and her willpower slip away

always an enthusiastic bed partner

the eager tremors of ecstasy

the sensation was both alien and exquisite

his hands moved with slow inevitability

his stomach twisted with the hard knot of need

her hands sledding over the muscles of his back

she could feel the slow warmth spreading through her limbs

virile intensity

all he wanted to do was enjoy her as greedily as possible

his hands burned a path down her bare back

the magic of his mouth and fingers overrode her inhibitions

was this love, or a convenient release of physical desire?

giving herself to him with sweet abandon

every curve of her body molded against his

his tongue demanded full surrender

his mouth closed softly over the flower of her breast

the butterfly play of his fingers searching for her nipples

he stripped off her clothes with speed but control

the fierce heat of him against her

the deep upward and downward heaving of her breasts

molten shafts of sensation ran down her stomach to her legs

his hands made heated paths up and down her body

the sensual heat of his naked skin

pure gasping passion

she molded herself against him wanting more

a sexual electricity sparked between them

she felt a painful ache building between her thighs

the burning sweetness of her hardened nipples

clamorous flame of arousal

an unspeakable desire

his hands roamed over her breasts with lust-arousing exploration

she felt his powerful male hardness against her thigh

his lips drew her nipple taut

moving against him, she reached down to caress him

she met the full force of his passion with an equal force of her own

the untold delight of his throbbing hardness

the heat spread through her

his hands moved magically over her smooth breasts

the soft firmness of one of her breasts just touched the side of his face

the man-heat vanished, but the pain remained

he ran his hand up and down the deep furrow of her spine

she felt the heat of his body radiating toward her

the rhythm of sex beating in her heart

exposing her lean muscled buttocks and legs

his hand on her breast continued to move gently

he proved to be the superior wrestler

his tongue demanded full surrender

catching fire from his flame

her fingers moved across the smooth sweat-slippery flesh of his back

exultant sensation wafted through her in heated waves

sliding his hands down her back to her buttocks

pulling her firmly into the spread of his legs

his hand roving down the back of her thighs and up again

his palms followed the curves of her breasts

the rose-hued tips were puckered with desire

wordlessly, she rolled over and put her arms about his neck

a leg stroked the back of her own leg, up and down . . .

the sound of sex was the only reality in the room

his naked body claimed her

fanning his fingers wide apart, he circled her breast

his knee moving between her bare legs

hunger rose and flared in her like a savage animal

she rubbed his calf muscles with the heel of her foot

the muscles of her thighs and belly flexed rhythmically

holding him at her nipples, she slid partially under him

his fingers parted the soft curling hair to stroke her

the incredible power of his surging body

rough, raw lovemaking

steadily her hand ventured lower

wrapped in glowing ecstasy

his knee moved to part her thighs

their bodies came together with the reverence of tender love and the passion of seduction

the giving and receiving made them partners in light and shadow

making love with a hungry intensity

firebolts of desire arced through her

caressing him with the instinctive movements of a woman who knew how to please her man

her breasts firm with aching arousal

his hands massaging the satiny planes of her stomach

she arched her hips to meet him

her body understood his rhythm

her virgin body was boiling at a feverish pitch

welcoming him into her body

interlocking rhythms

her body opened to him

her body ached with the promise of fulfillment

with each deepening thrust she trembled

wrapping her legs tightly around him, she pulled him into her

his thrusts were slow and measured

instinctively, her hips lifted in a sensuous invitation

his hands covered the triangle of soft, curling hair

her legs thrashed wildly

she lay paralyzed beneath him

she was tight but responsive

nearing a crucial juncture

the fires of expectation were out of control

the final explosion of physical sensation

a starburst of ecstasy, starting deep inside

the piston-driving strength of his body possessing hers

holding tighter, she wished the rapture would never end

hovering over her slender frame

abandoning herself to the spiraling climax

passionately she arched to meet him

steady thrusts of possession

patiently he brought her to the brink of climax

with a fevered groan he suddenly jerked inside her

taking her past naked desire to fulfillment

the moment of ecstasy exploding all around her

trembling from the world of wondrous sensations

the hunger they had for each other finally satisfied

a dizzying, uncontrollable burst of joy

the earth fell away and she went with him to that place of rapture, utterly consumed

sighs of satisfaction shook through his body

afterward, they lay in silence

he felt like a bird drifting on shafts of air

she crawled into his arm, snuggled there

just holding her through the night

they slept and woke and loved again

SLANG EXPRESSIONS

mere proof won't convince me

whatever it is, may he lose all use of it

attempting one of his rare excursions into humor

his joke fell as flat as a coffin lid

How long has this razor been in your family?

he made a play that marked a high in audacity even for him

I shudder over such a simple solution

Los Angeles's airport isn't exactly an obscure filling station

wearing his Flash Gordon outfit

getting a little long in the tooth

groupie mentality

the clown prince

about as lighthearted as a coronary

hand-picked for slowness

Thoom!

uh-ohhh

with all the blinding speed of a sloth on Librium

tart enough to pucker your asshole

I didn't even try to shave. I can't stand the sight of blood

Can I get a transfusion around here?

dirt-under-your-fingernails poor

possessed with the "gotcha" syndrome

she might, if the stars were in favorable conjunction, condescend to show you . . .

I'm just a salve associate

You comprendo?

about as popular as a tax increase

kick my butt

a chubbo

this is too heavy for me

I say this from the bottom of my mouth

we all have headaches, those of us who have heads

Texas excess

It is happening?

Bailiff! Valium . . .

numero uno honcho

Moosejaw, Montana?

a King Kong headache

it can put more topspin on your life

not cramping my style, killing it!

it would be easier to win a dog-sled race with a team of Chihuahuas than . . .

Mexican standoff

Now that you've lost control of this meeting, may I speak?

the gross-out factor

part of me wants to, but the wallet part of me doesn't

we want off this detail

as long as an elephant's pregnancy

Did I say that correctly, my love?

Ahh, Director of Intelligence Clouseau . . .

he has been cast as . . . this is dead serious . . .

are you going to hail to the chief?

my wife has a way with seaweed

it goes together like gin and marshmallows

all right, everybody, snap ass

not exactly a lunch-bucket type of crowd

he'd make a good lap dog

another chuckly frolic

looking for the total Gestalt

a huggybear

sleazy hucksters

as sexless as a china shepherdess

more dumb predictions than an astrology column

my fortune cookie is empty

would it be considered absolutely diabolical if I . . .

from then on, it was straight out of Hamlet

the flawed American hero

one of the lovable things about me is . . .

he came on a little, but . . .

everything she says is just bubble gum

a sassy street kid

his speech had all the passion of a list of engineering specifications

talk about relaxed!

nowhere situation

Mr. Inappropriate

go suck an egg

holding tough

punched his lights out

cheeky wit

he came from the stink pit of the earth

a human tranquilizer

pack your bubble gum and go

nothing like a little sexist humor to lighten the mood

No, seriously folks . . .

damn lint-picker

a tub-side chat

really peed off

Ph.D. in one-upsmanship

honorary rhino of the year

look that up in your Funkin Wagnall

that'll take the wind out of your tire

burger corral

to get them to act is like trying to push jello up a mountain

I haven't died. I've been repotted.

If you're ever out of town, I'd appreciate it.

his tank is empty

Are we on the same page?

that guy doesn't have both oars in the water

it absolutely blew the British away

interesting as a washing machine manual

you're making an omelet out of this whole thing

she has her black belt in mouth karate

Park your tongue for a second, will you?

I'm having a migraine over here

he bombed out of the race

you won't be sorry . . . bitter, but not sorry

you need more filler in your diet

Yes, your majesty

in sole command of the SS *Horrible*

sounds like something from fruitcake land

as fucked up as a Chinese fire drill

Beat it! Haul ass!

it made a row of zeros to stun the mind

the typical overstuffed banquet

it's not exactly country-club talk

she had the nervous system of a hummingbird

I'm ready to buy padded wallpaper

a modern battery-driven kid

you twit

Listen up, will ya?

a take-no-bull official

as tight as a dot

he just sat there, being terribly British about the whole thing

born ignorant and losing ground ever since

equal parts nerve and hunch

made a high school mistake

sleek as a walrus

neurotic bubblehead

protocol perfect

high-octane personality

management by hysteria

total airhead

not exactly one of the Three Wise Men . . .

Lighten up, will ya?

stone-age mentality

as important as national coconut week

Didn't you forget your red-and-white whistle cord?

It's not as bad as it looks. It's worse

as promising as an Edsel dealership on Three Mile Island

Go ahead. Ream me out.

clamping his teeth into a toughyouburger

You have a date with Kong tonight?

gooses him forward

as simple as Mother Goose

you arshloch

stay loose, baby

did a spinner

he's on a roll

making finger shadows on the wall

slotsy

they fired his butt

hang it in your ear

charged up like a filament in a light bulb

Would you like to come to my place and see my compact digital audio-disc system?

looking good, Mrs. James . . .

I need a pill

before they make you a saint . . .

the bystanders evaporated

it was a real tractor among perfumes

tah—DAH!

looks like an entry for the Gong show

it'd be easier if girls just came with instructions

feel bashed in

Smooth? I was born before whipped cream

a nut with an attitude problem

don't get in his space

this one really did it to us

my libido needs shoring up

The misery of the rich? Are you kidding?

sent his neighbors into a four-star swivet

soonish

get your hand off my behind

linger longer

a doomed but delightful affair

Cheesh!

For this I shaved?

naturally the police completely freaked

well, excuuuuse me

the patron saint of mediocrity

I don't give a rat's ass what he thinks

Have you thought of an insurance fire?

he looks like a landfill

scaaary stuff!

SLEEP

sleep came in a drift of roses

sleep pushing away teasing problems

sleep came nudging in among the old man's thoughts

these things had wrecked his sleep and terrored his dreams

even then her sleep was cruel

the men quit their sleep

again he fell into a shallow dose

he drifted in placid, dreamless sleep

withdrawing into a dreamless sleep

withdrawing into a vague half-sleep

the guilt one feels when he sleeps in the afternoon

but even then, her sleep was cruel

he finally slid into a thin sleep

drifted into a hazy, drug-softened sleep

his consciousness clouded with sleep

I sleep buck-naked

TRADE TAGS

a good night's rest that comes in caplets

stretch out on our mattress and leave the rest up to us

another open-eyed night?

our authorized insomnia dealer

if you can't fall asleep, try floating to sleep

a rocker designed for dozing

chiropractor-endorsed mattress

neat for napping

SMELLS

I smell sneakers

the rancid stench of the industrial plants

the oily fumes of diesel fuel

ozonic smell of rain

the smell of wooden packing cases, shavings and sawdust

I could smell her light, warm femininity

the fragrance of the flowers filled all of the universe

the zesty smell of lemons and oranges

the kitchen was full of the scent of boiled herbs

the amoniac smell of sweat and piss

a gust of her smell

there was a smell of low tide and crawling things

sharp, piercing carbolic odor

the scent of dust and hot dry earth

the lusty odors of earth and cattle

the clean smell of soap

TRADE TAGS

a sharp raisiny smell

the robust, gutsy aroma of Italian wine

is smoothly aromatic

a flavorful aroma with a hint of raspberry

clean, bone-dry air

an intriguing fragrance

scent yourself with a mist of spring

treat your body to a delicious all-over body fragrance

a sensually soft fragrance, like lilies

an atmosphere as friendly as its aroma of home-baked bread

an elegantly exciting fragrance

the bold masculine smell of leather

the just-showered smell that lasts all day

it smelled tart and fruity and full of vitamin C

a fragrance to match your moods

the scent with allure

To breathe in the crisp air of wintertime

the enduring scent of fresh flowers

a powerfully masculine scent

Your antiperspirant. Don't leave home without it

Ah! the unforgettable scent of Parisian nightlife . . .

No problem. It's unscented.

just one whiff and you'll be convinced

Does your after-shave arrive before you do?

SMILES

smiling in a controlled, unmirthful way

his lips smiling with cruel confidence

she grinned out of an overflow of well-being

a smart-ass little grin

the magnitude of his smile pervaded her

his smile was unlike anything she'd ever felt before

a lovely, wide, warming smile

a smile that reached clear to her heart

He smiled. It was a good smile and warmed her

she saw only friendliness there in his smile

a perfect keyboard of teeth

she laughed with her mouth and her eyes

the choked laughter and tears streaming down her face

He couldn't contain his smile any longer. He beamed.

she clung to me and laughed

a toothpaste smile

a rare, intimate smile, beautiful with brightness

she had a singularly sweet smile

gave a short laugh touched with embarrassment

smiling in the calm strength of knowledge

a lovely sleepy-cat smile

a pistol report of a laugh

it was a deep, honest laugh, good-natured and sincere

with an audacious smile

her smile was always a surprise, a warmth

he was tired of smiles that didn't cross the chasm to him

he grinned through clenched teeth

an oily smile

he could smile without changing his mouth at all

a pale, greasy smile

a flicker of a smile rose at the edges of his mouth, then died out

he smiled something filthy in French then . . .

lopsided grin

with the faint beginnings of a smile

she suddenly unsmiled

everyone had been trained to smile at all times

with a dry, one-sided smile

his smile fixed and meaningless

his smile was more like a wrinkle with teeth in it

he grinned, but the smile didn't reach his eyes

his mouth lifted in a menacing, sarcastic smile

her smile was so transitory that those who saw it wondered if they had

all he could evoke was a courteous smile and a friendly nod

a smile as hard as a car grille

the eternal smile diminished slightly

took a deep breath and adjusted her smile

he smiled suggestively

a secretive smile softened her lips

she smiled as though out of pity for him

she smiled, but it was incomplete

he smiled very nastily

a smile that transformed her face into pure sunlight

she laughed; a kind of trilling laugh of sympathy

the sort of smile that forced one to grin back at it

her smile was disarmingly generous

he smiled with warm spontaneity

a smile crawled to her lips and curved itself like a snake

her smile lighted her up from the inside, like candles in a pumpkin

SOUNDS

the talk wrapped around him like water around a rock

sounded like a crowded tunnel

clop of an axe

a smoker's cough that could rattle the windows

the snap of shirts hanging on a windy clothesline

there was no movement, not even the whisper of a sound

keening wail

the engine rose and rose, passing through a cry and into a
scream

the tinkle of ice cubes, a sweet sound

a miaowing wail from one of the children

far away a siren stretched across to them

the sound of food being scraped from a plate

a fountain splashed mellifluous sounds

the roar of absolute silence

an intense level of noise

the discreet rattle of a pastry cart

a sudden danger-whistle rocked him to his feet

the alarm went off, a high, shrill, piercing, frightening ring a series of dry, sluggish reports carrying across the hills

the sharp and brittle crack of weathered wood

through the roaring din, she breathed one word . . .

the sound came spiraling down

the raw burr of the whistle

the hiss of the broom on wet cement

with a disgusted rap on the table

drumming his nails on the table, making a noise like pigeons' feet on the roof

she was hearing a myriad of sounds . . . voices, murmurs, whispers

to the acid beat of the hi-fi

birds sang like power lines

a flat sound, as though someone in the kitchen had scraped a saucepan with a spoon

the sustained whine of an ambulance siren

unbelievably loud, its frequencies plucking the nerves in his head

his whole body seemed wedded to the music

the distant bell of a streetcar tolled its warning

the group emitted a collective gasp

the uncontrolled sounds of a crowd anticipating . . .

the blast ripped through the building like the thunder of war

the endless cries of the trains touched her ears

the noise stretched like a tightwire through the air

the ceaseless hum of traffic

brilliant ringing of the bedside phone

phonograph records that established a mood

the astonished silence

the applause rising, lifting in great waves

a storm of applause

the quiet of the night shadows

the hanging clothes made soft, snapping sounds in the breeze

a gray spit of steam

the duck-quack horn of a model-T Ford

the disquieting tick of plastic wrap

he could hear his heart battering against his ears

the muted crack of icicles

the rain hummed against the roof overhead

the roaring shout of the awesome storm

the screech of steel-belted radials

his Rolls whispered along, silent and smooth

nothing but birdcalls to break the quiet

hockey-rink acoustics

TRADE TAGS

thoughtfully designed to give you noiseless performance

the reassuring purr of perfection

styled for reduced wind noise

the increasingly rare luxury of quietude

as silent as a putting green

has your privacy been invaded by the sound of . . .

an unusual and exciting sonic experience

with strong tonal contrasts

a superbly atmospheric sound

the wistful charm of country echoes

crisp, clear, incomparably clear, sound of

Think about it. How much does the distraction of noise cost you a year?

turn up the volume, turn on the softness

you'll be smitten by its high-tech silence

the beep that could save a life

avoid the constant, nagging preoccupation of listening for . . .

Feel assaulted by noise?

Whisper in her ear again. Call France.

pleasant fool-the-mind music for easy listening

the soft purr of reassurance

Come to birdland. Enjoy a rare tweet

the steady thrum of efficiency at work

always afraid of what people would think

afraid to question what was written in the scriptures

she had only sensed love at a far distance, never daring to approach it

his tension rose a few more percentage points

self-protective habits

the impatience of a challenger

performance anxiety

about as relaxed as the locker room at half-time

with such terrible suddenness

with a quick intake of breath like someone about to plunge into icy water

lit a cigarette, inhaled deeply, hoping his bluff would fly

when she found the note, every nerve leaped and shuddered

she stood there as though fastened to the wall

his face tightened at the use of the past tense

she felt numb, as if her feelings were paralyzed

her antennae picked up the subtle increase in tension

adrenaline level began to rise

a nightmare beyond anything I've ever encountered

enough to give anyone the screaming meemies

fear like the quick, hot touch of the devil shot through her

fear kept him at the peak of intense feeling

a hard fist of fear grew in her stomach

her whole body tightened, and then she took a breath

fear of the unknown knotted and writhed in his stomach

she winced slightly as if her flesh had been nipped

the tension had reached a flash point

the sense of being inside a percussion instrument

she felt a whisper of terror run through her

taut with attention, gluttonously feeding on the words

nerves at full stretch

in a high stress situation, the adrenaline kicks on

nothing could calm her strained nerves

her heart went into sudden shock

she took a deep breath and plunged

confusing rush of anticipation and dread whirled inside her

a frozen, frightened thing in his heart

she felt a sudden chill

the smiled jelled into an expression of shock

they sat in stunned huddles, their belongings at their feet

he liked to think of such intrahate as "creative tension"

he had good antennae and was instantly on his guard

having mastered the terrifying prospect of living alone . . .

sobered instantly by the frightening possibility that . . .

a short time, no longer than a breath

insecurity was her constant companion

her heart thumped against her rib cage

all of her inner warning-systems went off at once

every nerve in him strung to perfect tune

a dark premonition held him still

waves of grayness passed over him

leaving the little man in a paroxysm of fear

his face betrayed a certain tension, a secret passion held
rigidly under control

at age sixteen, a study of hate

with a shriek no one there ever forgot

death in another guise came licking her lips

she threw her head back and screamed a guttural cry of
terror

he stopped breathing

numb terror

his body rigid, his fists clenched

a scream clawed in her throat

the scream seemed eternal

he came back to life in nightmare, flesh and blood

the scream chilled him to the marrow

sheer naked drama

the roaring of blood in her ears

a thunderbolt jagged through her

the blood slid through his veins like cold needles

it was a sight from hell

With every step, his jaw became firmer, his muscles tighter, his heart more eager. It felt almost like hunger

a look of half-startled wariness

she felt threatened by the strangeness

dismayed at the prospect of working under the aegis of a General

looking warily from one to the other like condemned criminals

he saw glances interchanged again

a creeping uneasiness at the bottom of her heart

she tried to keep the whole problem at a safe remove

it was different, vaguer, more chilling

like a breeze from a new direction

a slight, watchful hesitation

So dark out there. So dark and so forever

the sheer physical smoothness was alien, intimidating

a misty doubt

hazy warning

uneasiness spiced with irritation

a too well-controlled steadiness as if to conceal uneasiness

the effect was graveyard

assumed the role of self-doubted

restless activity

she paused for a moment, as if hesitant about saying her next thought

she shifted uneasily, not sure how to answer

a cold, hard-pinched expression on her face

the nervous flutterings pricking her chest

she felt apprehension and a faint though distant nervous anxiety

as anxious as a child who has stumbled on something he doesn't understand

I couldn't get over the obsessive sense of everything going wrong

bright and quiet but still listening and watching the door

suddenly aware of an unknown dread

no answer came to her, nothing at all

hid a thick swallow in her throat and turned away

he said, in torment

a feeling of having to hold close to herself, not to let go

she flinched, resenting his familiarity

a look, compassionate, troubled, and still

sensed the supercharged tension between them

for a second, no more, his arrogant face froze

the niggling guilt of her own inadequacy

they were both cross, both gnawed with anxiety

she felt everything go silent inside her

always there was darkness in his eyes

a tight place of anxiety in her heart

the unruly feeling of disorientation

haunted by the suspicion that . . .

she noticed she was walking on tiptoe

he said, after an agony of indecision

a suspicious sideways squint

the evening had that chopped, chaotic tempo that infected
all his hours

a day of gray unrest, discontent

assaulted by a terrible sense of humiliation

afraid of sharing her precious life

a man who was always restless for fresh horizons

walking the knife-edge of danger

a wave of grayness passed over him, a kind of dark
premonition

there was a strange, nervous unease about him

kept rubbing his tongue against the back of his teeth

she looked at him, waiting for soothing words

they'd never been more than careful strangers to each other

a fairy tale romance that seemed too fragile for the real
world

the uneasiness, without a name, returned

the days passed in a nervous blur

a haunting but somehow familiar place

performance anxiety

terrible gulf of misunderstanding

she was worried and wasn't sure why

friendliness so aggressive it was like hostility

VOICES

she tried to discipline her voice, to maintain complete control

his speech was warped by the whiskey

her voice was a high-sonic stiletto

it was a night voice, not a morning one

the coaxing timbre of his voice

a flat, inflectionless voice

her voice was light, trivial, like a thistle bloom falling into silence without a sound, without any weight

she said, in a parenthesis

with a little servant's cough

he went on with killing casualness

he spoke slowly, feeling his way

whispering close together in the darkness

clearing his throat of rumbling phlegm

a furious voice, lifted in a shout, stopped everything dead

her voice was quiet, tranquil, stubborn

with aggressive machine-gun speech

the breathy voice of an alcoholic

a carelessly drunken reply

liquid, loving laughter in her voice

an oily tone crept into his voice

a certain thrill of alarm in his tone

the tone of voice one might use to reprimand a dog

a glib, too-rapid way of speaking

an organ of a voice

his voice was stentorian, rumbling

a sweet edge to her voice

high-pitched and reedy

a thick, clotty voice with an uneducated accent

the total conviction of his tone

in a flat, inflectionless voice

his voice cracked with a sardonic weariness

the rich timbre of his voice

she went on, blithely ignoring the sudden silence in the room

he replied in a pensive tone

the voice was conciliatory, mesmeric

spoken in a clotted jargon

he sighed gustily and said . . .

His voice trailed away. He'd said enough.

the words hung in the heat between them

an empty tone

a "good old boy" voice

a fast hustler's voice

his voice was soft and eminently reasonable

he slurred some words between his teeth

she explains everything crisply

his voice was like a warm embrace in the chill air

a voice with the music of singing in it

she called again, too sweetly

his voice brimming with distaste

the quiet singing of a man working with tools

spoke in a low voice reserved for dreaded things

her voice had no strong intonations

she spoke in a neutral way, without inflections

barely managing to wheeze his way through the prepared speech

a bunch of yahoos

agreeing reluctantly, he made a grudging sound

a dark, liquid voice with restrained sexiness

with a brooding quality

a somewhat breathy voice issued from the radio

a terrible keening moan sprang from her lips

the endlessly redundant dialogue

a flat-as-Kansas speaking style

a sexy, sensational voice

it was the most purple language ever to cross her lips

his words were like the desecration of a temple

a spitfire tongue

he fired verbal missiles at the slightest provocation

her fine, reedy voice

a deep tobacco-roughened voice

her words had bite

his voice was a thin whisper

he uttered only disjointed sounds and strangled groans

his voice was soft and eminently reasonable

his words ran together in a velvet sound

his voice was like steel wrapped in silk

a voice as husky and golden and warm as the sun

her voice sounds like someone vacuumed the parakeet out
of its cage

her voice danced ahead of her into the house

the vapid, endless chatter

explained with limpid clarity and endless patience

a soft ghost-thing coming from a distance

her laugh had a hyenalike quality to it

a terse, vigorous voice

a powerful editorial voice

he had a gluey voice

he said, snorting

his voice as cold as his eyes

an accent with a singsong lilt

a voice like two sheets of sandpaper being rubbed together

an edge of desperation in his voice

sounded dismally defeated

top-drawer accent

the low precise voice of a New Englander

said between clenched teeth . . .

wistfully defeated voice

ominous inflection

whimpered like a homesick puppy

her voice was choked with sincerity

voice was controlled, almost tight

Her voice was cold. I was losing her.

his microphone voice echoed off the walls

a hoarse voice tinged with whining

her voice had the echo of a dead girl's voice

her voice was low, but the words whipped like steel
between them

tidbits he casually drops into the conversation like gum
balls in a quiche

a voice that could cause a hearing impairment

jumped out to the street and roared for a taxi

WEARINESS

breathed an exasperated sigh

like legal time, oozing so sluggishly that movement can scarcely be noted

the day passed slowly with processionlike monotony

wearily, he considered his existence

his weariness seemed to grow

she let her head drop against the steering wheel

her mind drifted into a fuzzy haze

nodding, too drained to explain further

watched the clock as it edged toward freedom

to him, salvation was getting through the day

with a touch of heavy-handed drama

his eyes were sandy and his bones ached

standing there in a pose of weary dignity

the trip was ennui plus

the ashes of his dreams

with a helpless wave of her hands

the malaise in him almost choked him

he was always conscious of the dull throb of grief in his mind

her heart literally broke, in silence
he slouched out, bleary-eyed and weary
the fastidious fact-checking department

PLEASANT

a quiet day after a whole week of wind

for a change, it didn't rain

June laid a warm shoulder of sun against the kitchen window

the evening air was as astringent as alcohol

an air current brought the promise of dawn into the room

the last spring snow had melted in the warmth of the day

the flag billowing out from its shaft

the wind was suddenly sweet, the air pungent

the air vibrated to the long drop of the robin's song

a smudge of sun dappled through the cloud cover

the sun warm over the country flowers

the sky reached out and over into the land

the primrose sky and the high, pale morning star of full summer

scribbles of clouds

marvelous swanlike clouds going over all day

a dazzling white blur of a sun stood fixed

the sun was proud in the white-blue sky

the sun rose, a peaceful burst of light across the misty fields

through the clouds dropped shafts of sun

the sky glared hot and blue

dawn broke like a plucked string from the horizon

the yellow day opened peacefully before her

clouds scudded playfully across the face of the moon

a Sunday-in-the-park-with-the-children kind of day

an intriguing combination of a brisk wind and a warm sun

Easter-bonnet weather

Trade Tags

the breeze skims past you down the open deck

blue-white ripples of water glisten in the sun

Unspoiled. Pristine and ever sunny.

What big blue skies you have!

the splendor of bold mountains and sparkling streams

500 miles of sun-drenched beaches

a clear view of the tall cliffs of ice and snow

the skies are cloudless from one horizon to another

at night a warming zephyr rushes up the hill

the air, brisk, invigorating, intoxicating

every morning the colors of sunrise paint a new day

great no-problem cruising weather

one of those postcard-perfect days

a winter sonata in white

an old-fashioned brisk English walking day

the clear blue horizon wraps around you

a brisk paradise of a day

an unforgettable flaming-orange sunset

at night the skies are a muted purple

a glorious day of sun and shade and summer flowers

a clear night view of the dazzle and glitter of the lights below

UNPLEASANT

the bawling winds

a hard wind blowing debris and pedestrians

the wild wind hooted

the air as cold and vicious as syrup

cold, white, ghostly mists floating aimlessly

the swirl of greasy fog

the lightning cracking the skies apart

blowing its damn foul winds and strangling rain

the rain, as sharp as a lance against the windows

the wind came sliding down over the world

the fierce, steady wind shrilled toward the valley

a wind rushed out with snow in its breath

the wind slashed and shoved against the crowd

continuous rain imprisoned them for days

strong enough for a force-ten gale

a breeze that knifed lungs and tingled bare skin

the lightning rips and dazzles

flesh-cutting snow

the cushioning silence of fog

his figure stolen away by the fog

his ears were tuned to catch the whispers on the wind

a fetid breeze broomed the dust momentarily

a snow-chilled wind that blew below her skirt

rain streaked the cab windows like tears

trenchcoat weather

bone-numbing cold

lightning hung to the earth

a heaven full of gray scud

blue arms of rain reached down from the clouds

it was cloudy, socked-in, no light from the sky

the mood seemed ill at ease

it was the kind of wind that roars in your ears after you've gone inside

a real wind that blows dirt into your eyes and hair and between your teeth